WARFARE

IN

THE MODERN WORLD

Julien Freund

WARFARE

IN

THE MODERN WORLD

A SHORT BUT CRITICAL ANALYSIS

Edited and Translated by

Simona Draghici PhD

PLUTARCH   PRESS

washington dc

This translation first published in the United States
by Plutarch Press, Washington, D.C., in 1996.

Originally published in France as
LA GUERRE DANS LES SOCIÉTÉS MODERNES
par Julien Freund
in **Histoire des Moeurs** vol. III, pp. 382-458.
Copyright in the French text © 1991 Éditions Gallimard,
Paris

Copyright in the English edition, preface, notes and index
© 1996 Plutarch Press, Washington, D.C.

Library of Congress Cataloging-in-Publication Data:

Freund, Julien.
    (Guerre dans les sociétés modernes. English)
    Warfare in the modern world: a short but critical
analysis/ Julien Freund; edited and translated by Simona
Draghici.
        p.   cm.
    Translation of the author's La guerre dans les sociétés
modernes.
    Includes bibliographical references and index.
    ISBN 0-943045-07-X (pbk.) (alk. paper)
    1. War and society. 2. War. I. Draghici, Simona,
1937-   . II. Title.
HM36.5.F718 1996
303.6'6--dc21   96-39242
                                                      CIP

CONTENTS

PREFACE

Many years ago, while analyzing such strategical factors as deception and surprise, and then again, while conceptualizing holy war sociologically, I became fully aware of the lack of a compact, no-beating-about-the-bush text-book on the sociology of war and implicitly of peace, that might become required reading, so to speak, for any student of conflict. As a result, I started flirting with the idea of compiling such a text-book myself, even at the risk of being ostracized by my fellow-sociologists who, in their exclusive love of peace, looked askance at anybody who dared to refer to war and warfare otherwise than to condemn them. Political scientists were more tolerant, though, but tended to be too prolix, sometimes vying with the journalists in offering the public thick tomes on one aspect or another of real wars, the arms race, or the pros and cons of prospective policies concerning national defence and the peaceful coexistence with other nations. All of them, though, would stress that their efforts were ultimately meant to put an end once for all to war by changing it into a negotiable and non-violent kind of conflict. Only the military historians agreed to disagree with the rest, but nobody would listen to them, anyway.

After some research on the subject-matter and a couple of synopses, I wrote to Professor Julien Freund about my intentions and at the same time suggested a colloqui between us at his home in Alsacia, at a date to be agreed upon. (An exchange of letters on the subject-matter in question would have been too cumbersome with its time lag between questions and answers, and so on.) His reply was not only positive, but what was more, quite enthusiastic. Nevertheless, the pursuit of other projects in the making took me away from the demanding work which the compilation of a text-book, however compact, on the sociology of war, would require. As I kept postponing the colloqui, Professor Freund, with the

generosity of spirit that was characteristic of him, kindly
sent me some of his articles on related topics, and eventually, a copy of his long essay on war in modern times, written
for the encylopedic history of mores brought out by Gallimard, the Parisian publisher, in his collection LA PLÉIADE.
Together with my notes and synopses, they were meant to serve
as groundwork for our date-still-to-be-settled colloqui at
Villé. It never took place: Professor Freund died on the 10th
of September 1993. That project of mine never went beyond a
a folderful of notes and Professor Freund's extract with his
hand-written dedication. Meanwhile, ill health and old age,
too, have forced me to change my priorities more than once,
and so doubtful of a successful completion of a text-book on
the sociology of war on my own, but still positive about the
need of a compact manual dealing with war sociologically,
I have decided to bring out an English edition of that very
essay by Professor Freund, instead. It contains everything
that I would have expected, and much more, from a work of
its size. In this way, too, a modest tribute is paid to
his memory, his intellect and his sagacity, worthy of such
predecessors at the University of Strasbourg as Simmel,
Max Weber or Carl Schmitt, to mention only them.

Born on the 9th of January, 1921, Julien Freund belonged
to the far end of the generation born between the two world
wars, for whom life was no cabaret, but a sequel of social
and political events that rolled them over with the inexora-
bility of fate and left an indelible mark on their ways of
judging and reflecting upon the surrounding world. Early
in life, he decided to meet events head on, with the exis-
tential earnestness which he never abandoned, not even while
sharing recipes for choucroute with his fellow-Alsacians, in
more relaxed times.

It is the acute perception and in-depth penetration of
facts and events, that also demand an ever wider scope for
the nexus of interactive forces, so characteristic of him,
that secure him a place among the classics of modern social
thinking, not only in France, but wherever the questions addressed by him find an echo and a reflex. Furthermore, a
native of Lorraine who became an Alsatian by choice, Julien
Freund knew how to make the most of his bilingual culture:
the synthesis of French, German and Alsacia-Lorraine civilization, which his personality embodied, lent his thinking

the breadth, ballance and originality that avoided the
pitfalls of provincialism and geopolitical boundaries and
met the challenges of an ever expanding theatre of events.
Although born several months after Max Weber's untimely
death, he continued Weber's tradition not only through
intellectual affinity and a close reading of Weber's works,
but also through steady intercourse with kindred spirits,
such as Raymond Aron, and actual students of Weber's, like
Carl Schmitt. There was no room for dogmatism in such a context, either, because the latter was lived and thought over
continuously. It was that reflective sensitivity that I found
so stimulating and reassuring on this side of the Atlantic
where sometimes understanding of wordly events could be so
limited, and superficiality is the condition sine qua non
for an academic career.

Julien Freund was also one of Gaston Bouthoul's associates
at the Paris Institute of Polemology, Bouthoul being among
the first modern social scientists to work out a consistent
sociological approach of the phenomenon of war with all its
implications and consequences, demographic and otherwise.
Then, as chairman of the department of sociology at Strasbourg University, Professor Freund succeeded in creating an
Institute of Polemology in that city in 1970. Besides, in a
world which has conflict for its key-stone, he not only re-
searched it and went on lecturing about its various aspects,
whether belligerent or not, but also published extensively
on such subject-matters as the political causes of peace,
violence, strategy, military as well as economic, the insti-
tutional evolution of warfare, and so on. In a way, the
present work is a summary of his interests in polemology.

He begins his WARFARE IN THE MODERN WORLD by conceptualizing war, in other words, by singling out those irreducible
traits that distinguish a human social action from any other
and renders it recognizable as war from the standpoint of a
social scientist, or a sociologist for that matter. Then he
sets those traits against secular notions in circulation
and the evolving social, political and economic conditions
of this century, providing the reader with more food for
thought regarding the on-going developments. To understand
how things have come to be what they are, Julien Freund
embarks upon a brief review of types of war waged along the

centuries, in keeping with various forms of government in force at various stages in history, taking the case of France as main illustration. He follows this political approach by a discussion of the technical aspects of warfare, in other words, tactics, strategy, command, armed forces and weaponry, only to end by an examination of the moral valuations to which war (and peace), both as a consequential collective activity and as an abstract and a legalistic notion, has been made the object of, through time. On closing the book, one feels besieged by a battery of questions, among which one perhaps looms larger than the rest: if the first half of the century was dominated by total war, both in theory and in practice, what is happening to the very idea of war nowadays, in the absence of a ballance of powers, as the United States, keen on preserving the status quo, use their own military forces as well as those of the United Nations for police work? The international 'peace-keeping' forces, so incongruous in their light-blue helmets, as if with their heads in the clouds, in the midst of local fighting irregulars, often better equipped than they, are a vivid example of the crisis of identity which regular forces everywhere experience in the aftermath of the application of the American doctrine. On the other hand, technology seems to have reached the threshold of diminishing returns, where misrepresentations by manufacturers of weapons and inflated costs put at risk one's own military personnel and make havoc of one's strategic plans. It is its open-endedness that invites the reader of the book to identify new trends and pinpoint the consequences. The book itself, conceived as it is in the light of continuous social change, provides the launching pad, so to speak, for more diversified investigation.

The English edition has not unfortunately benefited by the advice and clarifications which the author might have bestowed upon the translator. Hence my inability to identify some of the sources, such as, for example, those regarding the 17th-century French strategist, Furet. In order to comply with the requirements of the French editor, the original text had no footnotes, but only some sparse parentheses within its body, and a Bibliography at the end. As this edition is published with the college-student in mind, I thought it necessary to add not only notes at the end of the text, but also an index, though neither is exhaustive. In the process, I did away with the Bibliography following the original text, but inserted the bibliographical references into the Notes. Wherever possible, I substituted English editions for those used by the author. For the titles that have not been translated into English or the English translations of which are too free of the originals, I have used the editions referred to by the author. In the case of omitted sources, I inserted those which were most accessible to me while editing the text. Hard to find titles with no direct reference to the English edition were left out of the bibliographical references, while a couple of relevant ones were added. As regards the quotation of titles in the text, I must admit a certain inconsistency: wherever English titiles were available I put them in, but I also provided English titles for works that had never been translated into English, wherever the original titles were too long and complicated, like, for instance, those of Folard's writings. This was done to avoid a false impression of pedantry that might dispirit the otherwise eager reader.

All this work could not have been carried out without the solicitous assistance of the staff of the social sciences and the humanities reading-rooms of the Library of Congress, who have won my gratitude.

Last but not least, there is a special privilege that I must acknowledge, namely that of enjoying the gracious approval and moral support, granted to me by Mme Marie-France Freund during the period that led to the publication of this English edition of her late husband's opusculum.

Washington, DC
July 1996

SIMONA DRAGHICI

INTRODUCTION

Most people claim that they want peace, and even that they love it, yet in spite of it all, there are always wars, and often, they are made with alacrity. Jean-Jacques Rousseau thought that war was born of peace, or at least of the precaution which people took in order to secure a lasting peace.[1] In fact, whenever war is examined from the standpoint of causal pluralism, seeking both to understand and explain it, it surfaces that the will to peace or the search for it are often sources of war. That is so because one either wants to safeguard peace against the claims of others, intent on imposing their way of life, or one seeks to secure an undisputed place for a universalist notion of peace in the name of some religion or ideology. It is general knowledge nowadays that the advocates of a humankind freed of any kind of conflict and violence are by and large the first to promote a war-like stand under the revolutionary label, meant to impose the peace of their dreams upon everybody some time in the future. Thus, ultimately, war is held to be less unjust than it is claimed out and loud: it is the spring of the peaceful and virtuous order which one would like to see prevailing.

Proudhon, who did not care about the moralizing warnings uttered by the philosophers, preachers and social prophets, agreed without ado that war was a divine thing and one of the categories of our thinking. In his inimitable style, he even came to state: 'Heil to warfare! It is by its means that man, hardly emerged from the mud that had served as his matrix, reveals his majesty and valiance; it is over the corpse of a felled enemy that he has his first dream of glory and immortality. The flowing blood, the fratricidal slaughters horrify our philanthropy. I fear that the softness might but herald the slackening off of our virtue.To promote a great cause at the risk of imparting or receiving death through heroic combat in which the dignity of the warriors and the presumption of law are equal, what is so terrible about that? What is especially immoral about it? Death is the culmination of life: how could man, the free, moral and intelligent creature that he is, end more nobly? The wolves, the lions, as much as the sheep and the beavers, do not go to war against themselves: that remark was turned into a satire a long time ago. How can one not see that,on the contrary, the sign of our greatness rests in it? Admitting the impossible, had nature made man into an exclusively industrious and sociable animal and no warrior in the slightest, then from the very first day, man would have fallen to the level of the beasts which have no other fate but to flock together.... Living in an unadulterated community, our civilization would resemble a stable. Philanthropists, you are talking about abolishing war; watch out: you might degrade humankind.'[2]

Only God knows how many great thinkers besides have sung the praises of warfare. Jeremiah's lament comes suddenly to mind: 'For all, high and low,/are out for ill-gotten gain;/ prophets and priests are frauds,/everyone of them;/they dress my people's wound skin-deep/by saying,'Peace, peace.'/While there is no peace.'[3]

As a matter of fact, we are witnessing a present manner of expressing one's desire of and aspiration for peace that is remarkably bellicose.

Whatever that may be, if we take into account the successive condemnations of war and the vindications of peace, or the other way round, the glorifications of warfare and the appeals to violence in order to render triumphant ideas that, in principle, are generous and emancipatory, we must admit that it is hard to rid ourselves of value judgments whenever the question of war or peace is raised. Would a largely objective analysis be possible? One must bet on it. One must assume that lucidity and accuracy are possible if one wants to avoid falling into the trap of rival ideologies and propagandas. The very least we can do is to take pains to get a sociological understanding of the historical permanence of wars and the transformation they have gone through in the modern world.

I

SOME ESSENTIAL REMARKS

War is a social phenomenon that can be defined rather unambiguously, thanks to certain constant, characteristic features which it displays. Although constant, they are not altogether unchangeable. It is the very task of historiography, ethnography, and of sociology to describe the variations assumed by these persistent traits in circumstances affected by time and place. These characteristic features are the following:

1. Societies are either in a state of war or in a state of peace, without any room for a third state, save in the form of transition, an intermediate state between a war not yet acknowledged as such and an uncertain peace. Cicero referred to it explicitly in one of his speeches in the Roman Senate: 'Between war and peace there is no middle term.'[1] No dialectic has so far been able to overcome this dichotomy by defining a third state which would be neither war nor peace, meaning by that also larval warfare and festering peace. Indeed, there are dialectics that attempt to give us the illusion that in the future, under the effect of progress, humankind would succeed in overcoming this duality. In reality, all that they manage to do is to oppose a utopian state of universal and permanent peace to historical humankind, the latter being conceived by them as a kind of prehistory that has degenerated into an endemic bellicosity. Those dialectics do not put an end to the dichotomy of war and peace. They only attribute to one of the two states, namely to peace, an ideal dignity and an allegedly indefinite duration. This ideal picture is made possible only by depriving the notion of peace of its essential condition, that it is an exertion of politics in the same way as war is. Implicitly, these dialectics foretell the demise of politics, represented as the instigator of warfare. If we stick to the analysis of historical societies, without which neither sociology nor ethnography would be sciences, we see

that peace is a political matter as much as war is, and in such a way that by any prediction humankind will remain subject to the succession of war and peace, of which the already mentioned transitory forms are part. As long as man acts politically, in other words, as long as he is capable of violence, be it only as threat or probability, war and peace go hand in hand, so to speak. Once more Proudhon is enlightening in this matter: 'War and peace, which the simple-minded imagine as two states of things that are exclusive, are actually the alternating conditions of the lives of nations. They name one another, they define one another, they complete and sustain one another, as the inverse though adequate and inseparable terms of an antinomy. Peace explains and confirms warfare; in its turn, war is a revendication of peace.'[2]

2. Whether directly or indirectly, all modern nations have their origins in warfare. They have assumed the shape of specific and independent, political entities during warry struggles against the intentions of rival political entities, quite often accompanied by civil war. There is no need to go back and trace their history. One may argue against it by stating that certain contemporary states, say, in Africa, for instance, have won their independence as a result of negotiations with the old metropolis. In fact, those states were set up within the boundaries of the old colonies, the borders of which had been drawn by the old colonial powers as a result of military conquest. As a consequence, those particular states are indirectly based on warfare. Furthermore, the whole notion of border is materially necessary to the understanding of the idea of war and peace, respectively. As a matter of fact, the border may be a bone of contention as much as an object of mutual recongition in virtue of peace agreements that outline the space of each nation's independence, inside which their citizens may enjoy internal peace. It is in this sense that, for instance, the will to live peacefully, fully independently, according to one's customs, may lie at the origin of a war that is started out of the desire to free oneself of the tutelage of another nation.

3. War implies the presence of an enemy that may be defined as the other whom one wishes to fight for whatever reason.

Given the historical circumstances, it may be for the conquest of hunting grounds, the acquisition of booty, chattel or people (women or slaves), or because of the will to expand territorially or ideologically the space of an already constituted power. To go to war is to define one's enemy. Nonetheless, the war-generated enemy should not be mistaken for one's personal enemy who is the object of one's peculiar hatred. Carl Schmitt was among those who drew our attention to that aspect.[3] War is a hostile action of a group or community against another group or community regarded as the enemy. Thus war is not an individual, interpersonal event, but a social phenomenon. It is not a simple row or quarrel, opposing an individual to another. Jean-Jacques Rousseau, one of the very few people to examine warfare conceptually, has underlined this characteristic aspect appropriately:'If genuine wars are never waged between private persons, then who are those between whom wars are waged, and who are those who can really be called enemies? My reply is that those are public persons.'[4]

Thus the enemy may be defined as the public collectivity that is under the threat of war or against which war is waged. That is to say that to wage war is as political an action as is the stance of refraining from it. The definition given by Clausewitz in his book ON WAR is also to the point:'War is simply the continuation of policy by other means.'[5] In other words, war necessarily presupposes the presence of an enemy and the context of political activity.

4. All war is offensive, because it consists in attacking another political entity in order to impose one's will upon it. Indeed, the attacked community can wage but a defensive war. The response to a prior aggression is implicit in the very idea of a defensive war. Without attack, there is no defence. An altogether defensive war waged by both sides would be no war at all between them. Hence conceptually, war presupposes a confrontation, a clash or battle between armed forces, no matter what kind of weapons they use. Relatedly, Clausewitz is right when he writes that the engagement, that is, fighting, is the core act of war.[6] One cannot talk of hostility or war-like action as long as the political entities in question renounce all aggression and remain on the defensive. In many cases, peace resides simply in the decision taken by virtual enemies to persist in their

defensive positions in order to settle their differences by negotiation, for an undetermined period of time, or at least, until one of the parties decides to resort to aggression.

5.   War is both destructive and constructive at one and the same time. Generally speaking, one tends to remember the former aspect only, which is also the more spectacular. Not unlike Fénelon,[7] for instance, some people see in it a kind of absolute evil that discredits humankind. There is no doubt that in virtue of its immediate objective, war is destructive, being, as it is, a matter of breaking the resistance of the enemy and of imposing one's will upon him, often at the cost of frightening losses and extensive ruin. This aspect is so obvious that it does not need any further commentary. Notwithstanding, the cool-minded analysts of the phenomenon have come to recognize that war is not exclusively negative and nefarious. In their opinion, war is an evil not fully devoid of benefits for humankind. This explains why even such peace-loving writers as Kant recognize some good in warfare, in spite of it all. In consequence, war as such is exalted whenever it is waged in an orderly manner and is respectful of civil rights. The loftier the frame of mind of the people that wage it, the more they are exposed to danger and can courageously face it. On the other hand, a long peace is held to make the purely mercantile spirit sovereign, alongside vile selfishness, cowardice and feeble-heartedness, and so debases people's way of thinking.[8]

By and large, war is not waged for its own sake, but in order to set up a rule which is thought to be more just than the established one. Thus it appears as a means of dismantling the old order with a view to establishing new, peaceful relationships. As Hermann Stegemann once observed, one always condemns and dismisses this kind of destruction that leads nowhere as savagery or as the result of brutification. War has not become more atrocious in itself or more destructive than in earlier times, save that it happens to have to destroy more, because there are more things to destroy, and as a result, warfare has been amplified and intensified.[9]

In former times, wars were as destructive of fundamental and irreplaceable values as the modern wars. At the same time, it would take too long to count all the benefits and useful effects that have been attributed to warfare both

on a material and a moral plane. In passing, one may recall
that it helps regulate man's social activity and so acts as
a factor of equilibrium in virtue of Kant's principle of
the necessary 'unsociable sociability'.[10] It enhances moral
standards through direct experience of various virtues,
promotes progress and facilitates social mobility. Often it
is regarded as an essential element of the general economy
of human life, which by its nature also contains destructive
traits. Humankind cannot preserve everything lest it col-
lapses under the weight of what has been accumulated by
generations. Likewise, war intervenes as one of the destructive forces that stimulates man's creative capacities.
It is no doubt for this reason that war has always been
regarded as man's judgment of himself. It is likely to
satisfy his vitality as long as man is and remains the pro-
ducer of culture. Not a few of those who have written about
war have insisted on the cultural motive force that is inherent in it.

6. War is an instrument of man's domination by man, alongside such others as power, ideology, or economy. Here we are
not going to discuss the different ways in which domination
has been justified, least of all that which sees in domination a rational means that enables man not to fall prey to
the arbitrary desires of another, thus forcing him to re-
press his passions and turmoils. The simple historical fact
is that no philosophical or political doctrine has been able
to do away with it: there has always been a domination of
man by man in a variety of ways, some ruthless and implacable, others subtle or genial. Worth grasping, though, is the
sense in which war, as a means of domination, differs from
ideology, for instance, which is a means of dominating
minds by adhesion to a more or less coherent group of be-
lieves and aspirations. War is a means of controlling space,
given its political nature; in its turn politics itself is
not real unless it avails itself of a territory, no matter
its size. It is not simply a question of repeating what can
be found in any treatise of the military art or any history
book about the operations theatre, the various ways of
making use of waterways, forests and hills, or the diver-
sionary and encircling movements. Unless meant to finish
off a genocide, war usually seeks to control the space of
other communities. In this sense, it is a struggle to control

the space of the others, and indirectly, better to protect
one's own by reinforcing one's independence and freedom
of decision at the expense of potential enemies and their
capacities, weakening direct neighbours, or more likely
subjecting them. From this point of view, at any given
time, war rules the state of peace. Said differently, the
chances of peace are made conditional on the probability of
war. War starts when a nation does not accept to be invaded
by another, or be subjected to its control, when it refuses
to consent to the violation of its borders. That is why
nations are so sensitive to issues concerning their own
space. Khrushchev's reaction to the downing of the American
U-2 spy plane is a good illustration. Space is the Achilles'
heel of all politics, and consequently, of war, as the
ultima ratio, when the space is contested. No international
regulations have so far been able to eliminate this neural-
gic spot. There is no way of preventing a people from going
to war, if it wants to. Furthermore, if it has become convinced that it has been betrayed by its official government,
the people in question assumes the right to embark upon
underground struggle. Thus space is in a way the paradigm
of political independence, and consequently, of the speci-
ficity of a nation. Hence, war is not a game that follows
rules set in advance. It is a struggle in which the physical
and cultural existence of a particular political entity is
at stake. Between the hunting grounds and the security zone,
space assumes a wide range of connotations. It is under this
aspect that war meets one of the ends of politics: to defend
space proper against foreign threats. The other aspect,
which is the internal organization of space in order to
regulate cohabitation within its borders, in order to attain
the greatest possible harmony, is in the broadest terms the
task of the police.

7. War is a particular kind of conflict: it resorts to weapons, that is to say, means of attack and defence devised to
kill. As a matter of fact, there are unwar-like conflicts,
such as strikes, for instance, or the quarrels between
farmers over field boundaries, or still, the disagreement
between two power states, following the taking of hostages
by one of them, as it was the case of the staff of the
American Embassy at Teheran, seized by the Iranians, several
years ago. In other words, peace such as it has been always

known is no mere absence of conflict. Given the circumstances, any conflict may turn into a war, provided the protagonists have the will. Nevertheless, the belligerent conflict is characterized by hostility, that is to say, use of violence for deadly ends. It is precisely for this very reason that war cannot be compared to any game. As already said, a game takes place within pre-existing rules that define it. In fact, it is the difference in their rules that renders bridge distinct from whist, for instance. Likewise, rugger and soccer, cricket and golf, each have their rules, establishing in advance the criteria by which the winner is designated, which moves are permitted and which are forbidden, and quite often, also, the duration of the game. Moreover, a game may be resumed as many times the players wish; in other words, one may have as many rounds of any game as one fancies. The belligerent conflict, on the other hand, is of an altogether different nature: on each occasion, it sets up its own rules in an ascending order that aspires to the extreme, with a view to scoring a victory that would exhaust the enemy, and in principle, prevent him from resuming battle. Furthermore, the defeated is forced to accept the victor's law. A game brings face to face opponents who are rivals only as long as it lasts, without affecting their subsequent relationship; whereas war implies violent fighting between enemies with the intention of breaking the resistance of one of them by causing the largest number of casualties among the enemy's forces, or by devastating his country in order to paralyze life in general, to the extent of putting the survival of the enemy people both individually and collectively under the question mark.

II

THE MODERN NOTION OF WAR

It is in the light of the general remarks made so far that modern warfare should be understood, although two more points need to be added:

a. Given the fact that war is a struggle between two political entities, it is directly linked to their structure, that is to say, their social organization, their political constitution, their economic system, and their value system, in general. Military activity is attuned to the other activities. Consequently, the manner in which a war is waged depends upon the particular culture of the potential belligerents at any given stage in time. Thus war is as much the expression of civilization as are its works of art, its economic system, or its religion. Although in itself war is not something conventional, the way it is waged depends on each occasion upon the social conventions in force at the time.

b. As it is waged by means of weapons, each war is affected by technology and its development. Furthermore, the types of weapons used condition the structure of the armed forces, down to the tactical combat unit: phalanx, legion, and so on. Thus a technological analysis of war must take into consideration both the nature of the weapons and the organization of the armed forces.

It follows that if we want to understand modern warfare, we must examine it in the light of all sorts of social conventions, whether political, economic, religious, or what have you, as well as in keeping with material techniques and military organization, as two of the aspects of the human artifice in it. At a more general level, it may be said that military activity and warfare belong to the 'art' order. Put differently, they imply the contrivance of means and methods with a definite aim in view. All this in turn raises quite a few questions.

The first refers to the very idea of 'art'. Until not long ago, warfare used to be described as an art and so was the conclusion of a peace treaty. The titles given to some well-known treatises testify to it: Machiavelli's ART OF WAR or THE ART OF WAR by Jomini,[1] for example. As science invaded all the sectors of human activity, one started to talk of a military science, a science of war, as well as a science of peace. This new vocabulary is grounded in a certain tradition that goes back to the eighteenth century. The idea of a 'science' of war is already apparent in the Preface to Marshal of Saxe's REVERIES,[2] in the writings of King Frederick II of Prussia and in the Preface to Clausewitz's ON WAR.[3] Has thus warfare become an object of science in our times? Truth to tell, the writers just mentioned, all of them use the term 'science' in a broad, ambiguous sense, typical of their times, and above all, meaning reasoned discourse. The confusion arises as soon as the word 'science' is given the narrow, restrictive meaning of a group of propositions that can be demonstrated or verified and which in turn determine action. The issue at stake is thus to find out whether theory and practice, science and action may become one in such a way that one is identical with the other as far as presuppositions and explanations are concerned. This kind of assimiliation actually implies that the purpose of theory and that of practice are one and the same, and in consequence, their means are identical as well. As a result, the problems raised by science might be resolved by means of those posed by art, and the other way round: the questions of ethics and law, by means made available by economics, those of religion, by means provided by politics, or vice versa. In the last instance, no human activity would be specific, which also means that the question of war and peace would no longer be a matter of relations of force, but simply an issue made conditional on a broader theoretical knowledge. Said differently, the military man might replace the scientist, and the scientist might take the place of the military man.

If one wants to understand war scientifically, such confusions that turn warfare into an object of science need to be eliminated before anything else. Otherwise, a shot discharged of a rifle and a scientific demonstration are admittedly one and the same. Knowledge and power cannot be assessed by the same standards. Moreover, there is no universal competence to cover both theory and practice simultaneously. It would be an illusion to think it possible, which contravenes the very notion of competence. Warfare belongs to the category of action (practice) and not to speculation (theory). In concrete terms, it may be said that there is as much a military science as there is a medical science. Medicine is an art, because it demands savoir-faire, a certain deftness and intuition in diagnosis and the treatment of the illness. On the other hand, it is true that biology, which is a science, backs up medical activity extensively and helps it find its way amid uncertainties. Politics too is an art because it depends above all upon the flair and decisiveness of the statesman, which does not remove the need of scientific knowledge: sociological, economic and demographic. Likewise, the management of an enterprise requires other qualities beside those needed for economic research. Anything may become object of science, but the very object of study is not necessarily scientific in itself. Politics is not a science, though political science is, indeed. Thus, the fact that practice feeds on theory and theory feeds on practice does not mean that these two categories should be considered identical. Warfare remains an art: it makes use of decisions capable of an adequate use of military means in keeping with an intended objective. Such ability does not reveal scientific competence. The strategist, who nowadays works out his war plans based on the stock of nuclear weapons available to him, does not need to be familiar with the scientific principles behind their industrial production any more than Napoleon needed to know how to handle the scissors of a harness-maker in order to devise the plan of a battle.

Indeed, there is a science and even a sociology of the military personnel, alongside the military art. Not only is there a political science, but also a science of war, known also as polemology and which studies the military activity, its relations with the rest of society, the meaning of war in the context of human relations, the peace doctrines, and so on, all this according to the methods of scientific investigation. Its purpose is a better understanding of the phenomena of war and peace, and not the contrivance of means to a precise aim. Gaston Bouthoul,[4] for instance, only sought to carry on his scientific work, but never thought of casting himself in the role of a strategist preparing a counter-attack against the possible aggression of a hypothetical enemy. He did not want to win a war. He only tried to gain a better idea of the war phenomenon. Likewise, personally, while writing this text, I have no desire to assume the role of the commander in chief of the French armed forces. This is the confusion to avoid if one wishes to understand modern warfare, unlike a few military persons and some scholars who still fail to distinguish between art and science. Modern warfare remains an art as of old, although it resorts increasingly to scientific data in its strategic evaluations and its forecasts. Warfare, however, does not become scientific for that reason. In a way, the very conditions of scientific investigation are met whenever warfare is considered an activity that makes use of adequate means, and in consequence, is a matter of art above all.

This leads us to further questions. They are of two kinds, according to their implicit premises. On the one hand, anything may become a pretext for war, and on the other, war may drag in everything. There is no doubt that those premises are as old as warfare. Nevertheless, modern war brings out these aspects in bolder relief because it has succeeded in systematizing them. First of all, anything may become a pretext for a war-like conflict. Indeed, most often the reasons are political such as, for instance, the safeguarding of security guarantees or power expansion. Notwithstanding, economic factors have always played a considerable role, though, in the last analysis, hardly a decisive one. Religion has often ignited war, such as the denominational civil wars of the sixteenth century. Even the fine arts have fuelled war-like conflagrations, such as those staged by the iconoclasts at Byzantium in the eighth and the ninth centuries.[5] Revolutionary wars exploit ideas, and particularly moral ideas, such as justice, equality, freedom, to mention only them, on the pretext of liberating nations. Peace too may supply the motive of war. One may even say that war is waged in the name of a certain idea of peace which one wants to impose upon the others. Thus peace may generate war which is the opposite of the claims made by most legal philosophers that see in peace the antidote to war. Secondly, war may exploit everything, as it feeds on anything, on strong emotions, as well as on ideas or on interests. Clausewitz insisted on the importance of the nobility of character.[6] It is this mobilization of all human resources that has led to the contemporary notion of total war, set forth by Ludendorff who ultimately only radicalized the contents of a military text-book, PEOPLE IN ARMS by Colmar von der Goltz.[7] Ludendorff advanced the idea that war must, on the one hand, rally the entire nation, both its industrial capacity and its cultural and intellectual energy, and on the other, attack the enemy on all fronts, moral and material, by turning everything, even diplomacy or religion, into a weapon, thanks to the ideological effect of propaganda which must round off the purely military manoeuvres. WWII was an uncontested application of those precepts by both camps. The escalation to the extreme does not have only a military importance, but also a world-wide significance.

Another category of questions sets us at the core of the process that has so far stimulated the development of modern warfare. It is what Max Weber has defined as the increasing

rationalization of the different human activities. It is of
no use to go into detail about his explanations which he il-
lustrated by examples taken from the spheres of political,
economic, legal, artistic, religious and other activity.
More relevant to the matter in hand is his observation that
in this context warfare is not marginal. Weber himself never
elaborated on the matter. War has often been the innovative
stimulus of technological development which subsequently has
been put to peaceful use. Likewise, it has been the initiator
of organizational systems, such as strategy, and which
have ultimately been transferred to other sectors, like
economy, for instance. It is general knowledge that recent
wars have been as many opportunities to contrive or perfect
inventions that have altered the external conditions of our
daily life.

What Weber meant by rationalization, and here we follow him
closely, was the effort made to find the logically most
adequate means to attain a definite objective,[8] short of
incantations and magical means, such as prayers, curses
and other theurgical devices that have no direct and verifi-
able effect upon the progress of an action. On the other hand,
one should not fall into a dull positivism and reject all the
technically inadequate means off hand. War itself offers
evidence to the contrary. Pareto was the first to realize
that non-logical action must not be mistaken for illogical
action. He demonstrated it by recalling the conduct of Roman
generals before battle. The generals were fully aware that
the outcome of the battle was dependent in the first place
on one's ability to manoeuvre the troops in the field. Nonetheless, they were consulting the diviners before battle
because the prediction helped boost the morale of the soldiers waiting to engage in combat. Although inadequate as
far as the ultimate objective was concerned, the belief in
divinations could indirectly affect the chances of victory.[9]
Some additional remarks might be necessary in order to dis-
pel certain misunderstandings.

First of all, a progressive rationalization does not imply
a corresponding contraction of the area of the irrational
in the least. Rationalization follows a technical law of its
own, which does not impair the scope of the irrational. Thus,
contemporary warfare, however rationalized in its strategic
planning, may appear as a preeminently irrational act. In any

case, the ever increasing rationalization of the technique
of war has no debilitating effect upon the strong ideological
emotions, nor does it reduce the instances of thoughtless
behaviour. One may even set forth a proposition which is easy
to verify: an increased rationalization is generally accompanied by a consolidation of the irrational sphere. Hence a
second observation: it should not be believed that the desire for peace is more rational than the will to war. Peace
is more reasonable under certain circumstances. Various
records discovered in the Wilhelmstrasse archives at the end
of WWII show that the desire of the British and the French
to safeguard peace at any cost during Hitler's first incursions into forbidden territory only encouraged the latter
in his war-like schemes. That stand is known as 'the Munich
spirit'. After all, pacifism itself displays aspects that are
deeply irrational, as Gaston Bouthoul has shown: 'Even the
most exacting pacifists flirt with the idea of the possibil-
ity of legitimate battles whenever a war, big or little,
starts nearby or faraway. I must admit that I am worried
seeing our most sincere pacifists judge it from the standpoint of the belligerents. The pacifist confession of faith
boils down to demonstrating in favour of or against one
of the belligerents. The limit is to identify oneself with
one of them and demand direct participation, rather than
merely to express a sentimental empathy'.[10]

There are pacifist neuroses and psychoses as others are
bellicose. Moreover, in the pacifists' camp, one surrenders
to verbal attacks and to demonstrations that have as much
impact upon the preservation of peace as they have upon the
unleashing of war. I have shown somewhere else[11] that an army
of peace remains an army, nevertheless, because it conforms
to the rules characteristic of every army.

The astounding advance of rationalization coincides with
the advent of the Renaissance. It has transformed the military art and the methods of peace negotiation in the same way
as it has altered the conditions for the practice of the
other human activities. We shall talk about them further on,
when examining the conventional and technical conditions of
the evolution of modern warfare. Notwithstanding, rationalization is not the product of that era: it had already been
at work, though at a slow pace, in the preceding centuries.

If we take into consideration all the known wars in world

history, they may be divided into two categories, according to a typology originally devised by Hans Delbrück: one the one hand, the wars of annihilation, and on the other, the the wars of attrition.[12] Indeed, here we are dealing with ideal types in the sense given to these terms by Max Weber. In other words, the two categories do not exclude transition forms from one to the other: even the most ferocious war leaders, who won fame by the incomensurable devastations brought about by their armies, such as Attila or Tamerlane, and to a lesser degree Genghis Khan, did take into consideration the letter of the law and followed certain cultural inclinations.[13]

The wars of annihilation are as old as the world, so to speak, although nowadays they are likely to be called genocides, and are carried out in a more methodical way. They are swift and violent wars that give the combatants the freedom to act as they think fit upon the enemy population as soon as they emerge victorious. The war itself is spent in its conquests, because it destroys what it has sought to conquer. There are savage wars in which the soldiers spare nobody and nothing, busy as they are to sack, burn, pillage and kill. It was in such circumstances that the Babylonian Empire collapsed in the blaze set by the victorious Medes; that the Huns left only rubble and corpses behind them; Tamerlane turned the conquered lands to ashes, or the Swedes laid waste Alsacia and other provinces during the Thirty-Year War. In such cases, we witness the infernal, gruesome aspect of war, which can surface every time the fighters are left to give free rein to their murderous instincts, apart from a particular civilization that integrates the latter within its norms. It is easy to understand why this kind of warfare has failed to supply the groundwork for lasting political systems, despite the momentous success scored during the interval of apocalyptical victories. With the speed of lightning it conquers a huge space that it does not manage to control. The empire created in its wake is doomed to be short-lived, because warfare displaces politics and prevents the creation of lasting institutions, capable of weathering the challenges of the times. The very movement towards instant appropriation through conquest without restraints is self-annihilating, because it cannot install itself inside a possession as the decision-making centre of a regimen capable of bringing together space and time. By its very nature, it defies time. War for war's sake is self-destructive because it is not an end in itself. Unless it is inscribed within a broader cultural context, it exhausts itself speedily in the accumulating ruins.

As with other human activities, attempts have been made to regulate war, in keeping with the population involved, the period of time and the geographical space. Notwithstanding, war has remained a world-wide means of solving conflicts, albeit tamed into the ultima ratio, when the other means of making the enemy see reason are exhausted. Whether waged by so-called primitive tribes or by modern nations, warfare has been subjected to a codification or ritualization, which comes to almost the same thing, when one realizes that the religious symbols have been replaced by legal symbols. In both cases, pains have been taken to channel the drive of human aggressiveness, limit the ravages and contain the bloody and atrocious aspects of the act of war. It assumed the form of what Roger Caillois, under the influence of Montesquieu, calls 'the hushed pickaxe'.[14]Human dignity, so much talked about, rests precisely on the fact that despite the failures, man has never ceased to try and tame violence and its most explosive, collective form that war is. Indeed, human sociability consists in the perpetual effort, always threatened and always shattered, to limit the violence that kills. 'Historically', Caillois writes, 'war has oscillated between hunting and tournament, between slaughter and sport. The rivalry inherent in it directs war both to assassination attempts and to duel'.[15] We need to realize that, with all its ceremonial, the process of ritualization is a primeval or elementary form of rationalization.

The analysis of warfare confirms it: rationalization is neither uniform nor one-sided, contrary to the preconceived idea that only the irrational is formally diversified. So are the modern logical systems. Despite all the dialectics that would like to confine it to one direction only, rationalization is as manifold as there are spheres of human action. Each evolves according to its own principle of rationalization. There is no universal rationalization applicable to each and every action, while ignoring its end and the proper means to that end. It is not a sterile process that takes place in the void.On the contrary, it makes sense only in relation to the means that it resorts to and organizes in keeping with the particular nature of the desired objective. There are as many forms of rationalization as there are irrational forms, because rationalization is subject to the means-end relation, and this relation changes with each separate action. Ultimately, it is impossible to rationalize political action by employing the means peculiar to economy, scientific research, by means proper to the arts, or the other way round. Not only does the rationalization of warfare conform to the latter's own laws, but also it is accomplished differently, according to time and geographical space, as both sociology and ethnology show quite clearly. It is in this light that the wars of attrition should be analyzed.

Among the most current rationalizations of warfare mention should be made of rituals, whether of sacred origin or not, and of the organizational codes and techniques. Here I would like to insist upon the rationalization through codes, rather than rituals and ceremonies. In his remarks on Chinese warfare in the classical age, Caillois stresses the fact that at its fiercest, with massacres and extensive destruction, warfare occurred only whenever one of the parties was forced to defend itself against a foreign aggressor. On the other hand, in the case of intestine wars, a certain number of rules were conformed to, dictated as they were by humaneness, justice, order and prudence. One was prone to give up combat, regardless of the degree of preparedness and favourable opportunities made available by circumstances, if it was possible to subdue the enemy or the rebels by artifice or similar means. A victory obtained in that way was held to be more glorious because it was regarded as the triumph of justice and humaneness. [16]

At its limit, warfare tended to turn into a matter of deception rather than into a trial of force. In any case, a whole code of etiquette, although quite abrasive at times, was regulating the operations. In other places, the rationalization had a codified hierarchy of the social order at its basis: the warring function fell upon one of the classes. Among the best known examples, mention should be made of brahminic India with her caste of priests, her caste of warriors, and the other castes of the population. It was incumbent on the warriors alone to give battle. Although less rigid in feudal Europe, the principle was still turning the knights into warriors to such an extent that the rest of the population would become involved only in exceptional cases. Thus the military profession turned into the monopoly of a hereditary class. A genuine initiation ceremony accompanied the investiture with the arms of a knight, and an honour code defined the knightly conduct to be observed.The institution, no doubt, evolved along the centuries, because, at the beginning, any capable man could be invested without his social origins playing any part in it. Eventually, and in particular as a consequence of the crusades, whole knightly orders came into being, such as the Knights Templars or the Knights of St. John. The rationalization was rendered manifest by the pre-eminence given either to the cavalry or to the infantry. During the Middle Ages, the cavalry was predominant, although ultimately, it was flanked by halberdiers and by archers. It is easily understandable why under such circumstances, some of the confrontations were mere pretence, as attested by the very small number of prisoners and casualties on either side, and which sometimes could be counted on one's fingers. The Ottoman army was built up round a core of professional warriors, the janissaries, who were completely segregated from the rest of the population.

Finally, the methods of organization in keeping with the available types of weapons need to be mentioned among the most important forms of rationalization. Gradually, warfare ceased to be a chaotic advance of hordes, superior in number and in savagery. Among the best known types of organization mention should be made of the Greek phalanx and the Roman legion. In both cases, one deals above all with tactical units of foot soldiers recruited from among the citizens, reinforced by cavalry detachments. This is not the place to trace the evolution of the phalanx,from that of the hoplites in the Greek city-states (generally, an eight-row formation, for which the breadth of the front was more important than the depth) to the Macedonian phalanx, equipped with long-shafted lances and supported by a more numerous and better organized cavalry. Nor would the development of the Roman legion be examined here, from its beginnings based on conscription and the maniple as tactical formation, to its ultimate development into a mercenary army. What should be remembered, though, particularly about the Romans, is that they consistently adjusted their military organization in the aftermath of the reverses which they suffered on the battle-field, especially while confronting Hannibal: the setting up of cohorts, the creation of a supreme commander (Scipio the Elder was the first to assume that office), and later on, the construction of border fortifications in order to keep away those peoples that threatened the Empire from the outside. The practical creation of the office of supreme war commander was to be decisive for the Roman Republic during the times of Marius and Caesar. Eventually it was eliminated in order to make room for the Empire. A detailed examination of the evolution of such an army as that of the Romans, for instance, would reveal that the desire for an ever increasing efficiency was the motive force of its rationalization. On the other hand, the weapons remained the same throughout: the lance, the sword, the sling, the bow and the pike, while the protective equipment consisted mainly of shield, helmet or the armour (the breastplate, to which in the Middle Ages the harness for the protection of horses was added). The few inventions of the period, such as the war machines and the Greek fire were essentially defensive devices, and as such, had no decisive impact upon the conduct of war. It was only during the Renaissance that rationalization picked up speed thanks to the newly devised weapons that increased the strictness of the military order, and eventually altered the relation between man and warfare in a radical way.

III

THE CONVENTIONAL ASPECTS OF WAR

Given the direct relationship between warfare and politics, in the sense that war is one of the means of politics in pursuit of its objectives, there is no wonder that one of the first positive analysts of political action at the beginning of the modern age, Machiavelli, was a remarkable theoretician of the new kind of war, as well. His approach is not flawless, and a few things may be held against him, such as his omission of the issue of military discipline. Although a great admirer of the Roman Republic, he failed to grasp the fact that the Roman legion had not been merely a tactical unit, but also the result of individual self-control and the discipline of the military formation one belonged to. It is a strange oversight on the part of someone like him, who put such a high price on virtù. It was Justus Lipsus who rounded off Machiavelli's military doctrine by underlining the importance of the human factor and of the indispensable discipline. He did it in his treatise entitled DE MILITIA ROMANA, which was printed in 1596.[1]

Machiavelli favoured the formation of a people's or national militia, the expenses of which were to be covered by the state out of its revenues, and simultaneously, the dismissal of mercenaries. Stranger still is the priority which he gave to the infantry over the cavalry, associated by him with the feudal tradition. In his opinion, the infantry was better served by the conscription of citizens, which had been the strength of the Greek phalanx and the Roman legion. Finally, even more unexpectedly, he exhorted the militia to adopt a new tactic, a new way of displaying its combat units on the battle-field. Eventually, as it happens with any innovative idea, Machiavelli's did not seem attractive to his contemporaries. Besides, the fact that the Florentine militia organized by Machiavelli proved a failure was not encouraging either. Nevertheless, it was only a temporary setback; the idea regained its appeal and with time, it spread everywhere.

In the Preface to his ART OF WAR, he expressed his regret for the contempt in which the profession of arms was held, although the presence of an army was the unavoidable condition of the survival of a nation. He went on to say that a nation needed to pay particular attention to its military organization, lest it was prone to lose its freedom and its sovereignty. To recruit its citizens for military duty was unavoidable: they, the citizens, were aware of the risks they were running in case of defeat, whereas mercenaries were motivated by their personal interests only. Moreover, any oversight could not be corrected later on, during hostilities.[2] Machiavelli's analysis includes practical details such as the control of space. Arguing from the point of view of the conditions of contemporary warfare, and following the classical writers closely, he suggested to the prince to go hunting, in order to become familiar with the features of the surrounding region and be able to manoeuvre effectively, when his country was attacked.[3] It is in the spirit of his writings that I intend to review the evolution of war and peace against the conventions which eventually marked the joint development of war and politics. Machiavelli, after all, knew like none other to free political action from any ethical presupposition and ideology in his positive, and one may say, scientific inquiry.

STATE WARS

It has already been emphasized that the structure of the political entity at any given time conditions its wars, both their type and the ways they are waged. The form of the political entity bequeathed to the Western world by the Renaissance is the State. Warfare would change with the appearance of the modern State. Indeed, the State grew roots in Europe only gradually, in the aftermath of a slow and often-interrupted progress. Some nations adopted the new organization before others: England, France and Spain preceded Russia, Germany and Italy in this respect. Let us take the case of France. The road to statehood was long and winding. The policy pursued by Louis XI served as preamble, as his plan was to place all the territory, which in his opinion represented France, under a sole and undivided authority. That explains his campaigns against Charles the Bold and his hostility against the feudal nobility, keen on defending their local powers and privileges. His will carried with it some other initiatives, such as the introduction of a moral, rational administration. One of the characteristic features of the latter was the immovability of the judiciary. Given the subject-matter of this essay, it would be inappropriate to insist on this aspect. What is of primary interest is the new policy promoted by Louis XI's successors. Before his time, France had been the object of her neighbours' greed and so she had been a theatre of raids and invasions. Most of the battles had taken place on its territory, whether at Bouvines or the many places that saw combat during the Hundred Years' War. Nonetheless, the French kings wanted to go outside the boundaries of their realm and wage war abroad, as for instance, in Italy. It was with the advent of Francis

22

I that a genuinely permanent army came into being, which also meant the rehabilitation of the infantry. Until then, the cavalry had been the arm of choice, to the point that it had been 'the war ordinary', whereas the infantry had been an auxiliary arm, known as 'the war extraordinary.'[4] It was the Swiss infantry that initiated the new tactics, soon to be immitated by the Spaniards and the French. Roger Caillois was right to stress the fact that the new prestige of the infantry contributed to the emergence of the modern idea of democracy.[5] While the new idea of the State conditioned warfare, the opposite is also true, namely that its new methods equally influenced the gestation of a new political spirit. In the sphere of human interaction causality is mutual: everything is conditioned by what it affects.

Machiavelli sensed the new development, although the Reformation and the Wars of Religion did cause a temporary setback of his anticipations. During the Wars of Religion, faithful to their traditional political routine, England and Spain tried to get a foothold in France, but without success, because that country had become the bulwark of the new concept of State, which in the aftermath of their failure, both England and Spain took over for their own profit. What I am suggesting here is not to remake history, but rather to reread it. Without going as far back as the reign of Philip the Fair or to Joan of Arc, it is not far-fetched to point to Louis XI as the one who took the practical steps in the direction of a new doctrine of political unity, and which was later elaborated by the theoreticians as the doctrine of sovereignty. The most outstanding among the latter were Jean Bodin,[6] Loisel, Coquille, L'Oyseau, and eventually, Hobbes.[7] Henry IV benefitted against his will, so to speak, by the innovation of the political experts of the time, better known as 'the politicians'. Richelieu was the one to put into practice the theoretical intuitions of the politicians, and so handed them over to us. He may be considered the founder of the modern State because with his political flair he was capable of drawing to their ultimate conclusion the sayings of the jurists, including the idea of enemy, which is fundamental to each and every war.[8]

All in all, Richelieu's innovations represent a turning point in the practice of politics and as far as the rules of modern warfare are concerned. He was never a general, but in his quality of politician aware of the emerging trend, he transformed the customary idea of warfare, drawing from the practical changes brought about by earlier monarchs, and the opinions of the politicians with their legal training. The Wars of Religion and later on the Fronde were as many opportunities for the nobility to try to win back their old authority and privileges, on the ground of a theological quarrel. Richelieu's merit was to have grasped that sovereignty, understood as 'absolute power', according to Bodin's definition, [9] demanded the monopoly of violence, in order to turn it into one of the attributes of the legitimate State. The consequence of such a monopoly was that from then on, the sovereign alone had the right to wage war or negotiate peace. [10] All that explains the ruthless struggle carried on by Richelieu against the 'Greats', and the principle of joust and private war, persisting in the form of the duel, on the one hand, and on the other, against the Protestants who were holding various fortified places inside the realm, such as the town of La Rochelle, where an autonomous jurisdiction prevailed, capable of challenging State sovereignty and the king's authority. Simultaneously, the notion of enemy acquired a new meaning. The monopoly of legitimate violence, linked to the idea of sovereignty, excluded the internal enemy, or in other words, the use of violence in private contestations, whether political, hereditary, or religious. The State alone had the right to resort to violence. Thus only the external enemy was left, and as a result, warfare was further restricted because it could take place only among sovereign States acting as they did as public powers. This new concept of warfare also required a strict delimitation of the territory over which the State ruled as sovereign. Hence the policy of what was then called natural boundaries. It led to a distinction which eventually would become of capital importance to Europe's political sphere as a whole, namely the distinction between internal affairs, a matter for the police, and foreign affairs, the means of which are diplomacy and the army. Its normal and rational conclusion was the creation of a ministry for foreign affairs. Warfare too was assuming a new meaning. It ceased to be an internal adventure, left to the feudalists' discretion, and as such, an enterprise subjected to the hazards of whim, in order to become the means of recovering and defending the borders of the State in its entity. The campaigns launched by Louis XIV in Alsacia, Franche-Compté or in Roussillon were but the practical application of this new political will, though it is true, not without residual aspects, of which the Wars of Succession were full, resembling islets of tradition in the river of the new strategy, so to speak. Eventually, the king came to represent the absolute sovereignty on the territory of the State, to the extent that the local or provincial administration of the intendants derived its authority from the powers conferred by the king to his appointees to the corresponding offices.

After all, in all his war-like and administrative undertakings, Louis XIV was but the astute executor of the kind of politics which had been initiated by Richelieu, even to the point of embodying it (consider the words attributed to him:'I am the State"'). The most daring idea that helped disrupt the new development, as a logical consequence, should be credited to the luminary, whose other merits are ignored, probably because he fell out of favour with Louis XIV before his time. I am talking about Vauban whom the king failed to understand, and who still awaits to be rehabilitated by the historians.[12] He knew how to draw the military and political consequences of the new orientation. His strategical innovations are better known by far: the construction of fortifications all along the natural borders is one of them. He had the astounding idea of reconciling the military requisites with the political intentions, which after all is the groundwork of any strategy. He did it by endowing the country with an overall system of defence meant to dissuade any possible aggressor, but also to serve as base in the case of an offensive war. He did manage to build quite a few fortresses himself. Besides, he is held responsible for a number of tactical innovations, too, such as, for instance, the cross fire, the ricochet, and the bayonet attached to the rifle-muzzle.[13] Nonetheless, what apparently brought his fall was his prediction about the transformation of State wars into national wars.

The State is an institution essentially juridical and bureaucratic, short of an affective content. Vauban's principle was that the inhabitants of a State would not defend its territory, unless they had something worth defending from the point of view of their interests or of their affectivity.

Whatever the technical and material means available to the combatants, they would be of little use as long as the soldiers had no concrete and tangible reason to do battle. Vauban used that principle as the premise of his blueprint of the royal tithe. In the latter, he insisted on the human factor in the overall context of the subjects' situation inside the country. He advocated a sole tax, calculated on the basis of a census. Essential in that work is his foresight that an institution as abstract as the State would remain vulnerable militarily as long as the feelings and the interests of the population are disregarded. Later on, the concept of the Nation would provide the notion of the State with the missing emotional factor.

A similar concept had already been set forth in England, several decades earlier, during the Civil War.There, religion had been the main support of that war, contrary to what was happening in France. A people's army, under Cromwell's leadership, came into being by fighting the traditional army. Soon enough, though, the new army turned into a political power. New claims made themselves heard, among them the social demands of Lilburne's Levellers and Winstanley's Diggers.[14] Indeed, the partisans of either remained a minority, but still, they managed somehow to provoke social agitation within the army ranks. The Diggers were also among the first on the eve of the modern era to advocate a community-like society, based on equality, and which the later communist ideology would inherit. As a result, Lilburne's and Winstanley's principles of action would continue to exert their influence despite their military defeat. The French revolutionary army of 1792 would eventually display a similar frame of mind.

The State war had as objective to safeguard sovereignty, rectify borders, and only seldom, to pursue conquest. Exceptions were the wars waged by the Swedish king Charles XII in Russia, and by Frederick II of Prussia in Silesia. Indeed, in the eighteenth century the number of military actions was very high, but blood-shedding was not characteristic of them. It was the era of 'the lace wars', which corresponded to the so-called 'cabinet politics'. At the time, the military art consisted mostly of intricate manoeuvres meant to force the enemy to back out and acknowledge his inferiority without delivering any large-scale battle. It all rested on tactical

harassment. It was a kind of 'economy warfare', of which the
campaign carried on by the Marshal of Saxe in Belgium is an
appropriate illustration. He besieged Namur while the Austrian army stationed in the Netherlands was trying to come to
that town's aid. By skilful manoeuvres, the Marshal blocked
the advance of the enemy in the Ardennes in a way that forced
the Austrian army to back out in order to avoid an ambush,
and return to base. Namur surrendered as a result. One of the
contemporary war theoreticians, Heinrich von Bülow, was still
writing in 1799, on the eve of the national, revolutionary
wars: 'If one finds oneself constraint to give battle, it is
because mistakes have been made'.[15] Others saw in that manner
of handling the army an opportunity to wage war against war.

Indeed, this kind of warfare can be understood only in the
social and political context of the period. As already said,
the spirit in which politics was practised was that of cabinet negotiations, which is to say that war-like manoeuvres
were meant above all to support the negotiations going on
between chancelleries. After all, the act of war proper was
considered secondary to negotiations. It should not be forgotten that it was an era which witnessed the zenith of legal
thinking, the omnipresence of which was behind the advocacy
of a law of war. Suffices to mention such attempts as Grotius' DE JURE BELLI AC PACIS,[16] Pufendorf's CIVIL AND NATURAL
LAW,[17] Burlamaqui's PRINCIPLES OF POLITICAL LAW[18] and Vattel's
CIVIL LAW, above all. [19] The idea of war was made part of the
context of reason and of the Enlightment, in general. Vattel
was writing that if people would always be reasonable,
they would only fight with the arms of reason. Justice and
natural equity would be their rule or their judge. The ways
of violence were sad and unfortunate means against those who
despised justice and refused to listen to reason.[20] Voltaire
echoed this attitude by remarking the primacy of intellectual
criticism over political power:'There is not one among these
critics', he wrote in the Supplement to his PHILOSOPHICAL
DICTIONARY, 'who does not think himself to be the judge of
the universe, listened to by the universe'.[21] Even Frederick
II of Prussia found it necessary to draw the distinction
between everyday morality and the requisites of politics in
the Preface to his HISTORY OF MY TIMES.[22] In that age, criticism was held to be the genuine weapon.[23]

This general, intellectual climate had various effects upon

the concept of war and upon the status of the army. It was
during this period that the first efforts to humanize warfare came to be recorded. Louvois [24] founded the first military hospitals and set up the commissariat service capable
of supplying the soldiers with the necessary victuals.
In that way, they were no longer forced to steal in order
to eat. It was also during that period that the Hotel of
Invalids was built in Paris as a retreat for old soldiers.
Such initiatives in turn exerted a considerable influence
upon the very conduct of military operations. Thus, for instance, the system of campaign depots that stored the food-
stuffs for the troops conditioned the manoeuvring abilities,
rendering the manoeuvres more cumbersome. Warfare became
above all a matter of destroying the enemy's communications lines, in order to render him harmless. Rather than
defeating the adversary on the battlefield, one tried to
force him to acknowledge defeat, following a series of feints
and advances.

The first standing armies were constituted during that
period under the mandatory requisite to lodge the troops in
specially erected quarters when not on campaign. This latter innovation was of historic importance. The army's existence ceased to coincide with duration of the war alone:
its soldiers went on living and drilling together during the
period of peace. Military instruction and discipline became
the rule, and turned Frederick II of Prussia into a discipli-
narian of the strictest kind. Army maintenance became an
economic question in the context of the incipient science of
political economy. The requirements of standing armies were
onerous, and that is the reason why the number of their effective soldiers was low and why the monarchs had no interest
in wasting their military forces on the battle-field. Hence
the establishment of a military administration, so insist-
ently advocated by Louvois. Besides, the soldier's trade was
turning into a professional career, according to the new
principle of the division of labour. The standing army exerted still another important impact, in breach of the rowdy
habits of the old soldiery: the institution of regular troops,
clothed in specific uniforms, as well as the now classic
division into battalions, regiments, and so on, each troop
being made distinct from any other by its typical uniform.

The notion of war essentially as a series of manoeuvres,

the aim of which was to constrain the enemy to withdraw
without battle, if possible, induced the military commanders
to turn their attention to and reflect on tactical questions.
The immediate result was the publication of the first books
on modern-time strategy. The Frenchman, Chevalier Folard
was among their authors, and his NEW FINDINGS ON WARFARE IN
A DISSERTATION BY POLYBUS and COMMENTARIES ON THE HISTORY BY
POLYBUS became the bedside-table books of Marshal of Saxe
and of King Frederick II of Prussia. [25] There was even an extensive debate between the supporters of 'the thin order'
and the advocates of 'the thick order', which later on continued on the issue of 'the slanting order'. The matter was
to find a solution as to the places to be assigned to the
infantry, the artillery and the cavalry. All those books were
strictly technical, and so they are relevant to the history
of modern strategy. They made no effort of conceptual reflec-
tion on the very phenomenon of war.

Concomitant with the war operations which more often than
not were mere military parades,[26] diplomacy too became subject
for rituals and ceremonies, as exemplified by the conclusion
of the treaty of Westphalia. Eventually, the negotiations
would lose their festal character. To a degree, one may speak
of a sort of political marivaudage during that age. [27] It
was also at the time that alongside a war minister, like
Saint-Germain in France, a minister of foreign affairs,
like Vergennes, made his appearance at the head of a whole
administrative organization, because by then the appointment
of permanent ambassadors abroad, one of Machiavelli's initiatives, had been generalized.

That stalemate in the conduct of war was only relative,
though, because it was during that interval that the military
and diplomatic institutions that would prevail in the nine-
teenth century were born. The creation of standing armies has
already been mentioned, and to it one should add the rede-
ployment of the artillery, on Gribeauval's initiative,[28] and
the reorganization of the navy on the eve of the American War
of Independence. Thus everything was already in place at the
end of the eighteenth century, when Europe would be ravaged
by national and revolutionary wars. The very doctrine that
spelled out the new war formula had already been completed,
particularly through the contributions made by King Frederick
II of Prussia, and by the French Count Hippolyte de Guibert.

Frederick II deliberately cast away the prudence shown by the generals, his contemporaries. He even worked out the new rules of warfare. In his opinion, a project of one's own had to be adhered to until its completion, because in that way, one would reach out farther than the generals who usually were waging war haphazardly. He was hostile to the manner in which war was waged during his life-time, preferring the dare-devil of a general who purposefully took the risk of a confrontation to the advocates of a systematic defence, because the former had everything to hope for, his expectations were not circumscribed. Frederick II considered the best those battles in which the enemy was reduced to the condition of giving battle against his will. Thus to force the enemy to do what he did not want to became one of the rules of warfare. Essentially, Frederick II of Prussia did make the connection between politics and warfare: it was his recommendation not to go into battle only with the intention of defeating the enemy but rather in order to achieve one's plan.[29] As a result, he reorganized Prussia's financial system, as well as the transportation network and the supply system, or in other words, he modernized logistics.Likewise, King Frederick II became an expert in propaganda and managed to attract the best minds of Europe to his court. He reorganized the celebrated Berlin Academy, the new president of which was Maupertuis, a French mathematician and astronomer.

Hippolyte de Guibert perfected Frederick II's work by giving it such dimensions that are still striking by their modern character.[30] Above all, Guibert is known as the author of a treatise entitled GENERAL ESSAY OF TACTICS, which saw the light of print in 1772.[31] Both Washington and Napoleon were impressed by it. Guibert's main premise was that the power of any State derives from its own power, and its prosperity, from its own prosperity. His advocacy was in favour of power politics of which warfare was an essential resort. He dismissed the elementary tactics of the distribution of orders at the level of battalions or regiments, and instead, turned spokesman for grand tactics, which was what strategy was called at the time. The latter came to represent the overall view of a commander in chief who no longer reasons exclusively in military terms, but takes into consideration political, economic, administrative and technical data. The problem facing him is to put an army in motion by taking into account all the possible givens. It is still worth reading Guibert's ESSAY and his last book, entitled ON THE PUBLIC FORCE EXAMINED UNDER ALL ITS ASPECTS, and printed in 1790, as also his letter of the 10th December 1789, addressed to the National Assembly, just a few months before his own death at forty-seven. He took to task the bourgeois deputies on the subject of the popular class: 'You made them bitter, you aroused them and you armed them, and you think now that you can revert this unleashed torrent to its bed peacefully. You think that your laws can serve them as their guide, and that in their turn, they will not want to draw any profit out of a revolution whose tools you have made them into. ... Think of it'.[32]

Thus the problem which the national and revolutionary wars would raise was already clearly stated before their advent.

NATIONAL AND REVOLUTIONARY WARS

One may be taken aback by such a typology that places national wars alongside revolutionary wars in one and the same category. Despite all appearances, it is not an arbitrary categorization; far from it. First and foremost, it facilitates the understanding of another phenomenon, to be discussed further on, namely total warfare. It is true that, by and large, present-day literature tackles each of them separately, thus encouraging the inference that national wars constitute a particular type of warfare. Indeed, there have been national wars which remained alien from any revolutionary movement, such as the Prussian-Austrian war of 1866, for instance. The exceptions confirm the rule. As a matter of fact, most of the national wars since those of the French Revolution either have had a direct, revolutionary origin, included a decisive, revolutionary event, such as the Paris Commune of 1871, or ultimately, unleashed a revolution. The relationship is also corroborated by the pseudo-revolutions in Eastern Europe in the aftermath of WWII. There is no doubt that the relation between national and revolutionary wars is not logically necessary, although historically, their correlation is consistent.

In fact, the Nation displays a new political and social context, in contrast to the State, although the State per-

31

sists in the modern Nation through its bureaucratic rationalization and its division into various public services.
This is not the place to go into detail about the relation
between State and Nation, and examine the nineteenth-century
phenomenon of the Nation-State, or to show that in certain
cases, such as that of France, the State preceded the formation of the Nation, whereas the opposite happened in Germany
and Italy, where national revendications served as basis on
which the new states were erected.

In France, the idea of Nation first assumed political significance during the latter half of the eighteenth century.
Subsequently, it served as a lever to the policy pursued by
the French Revolution. What interests us here, however, is
the contribution made by the concept of Nation to the appearance of a new type of warfare. Above all, the State represents
the abstract and legal structure of a political unit. The
Nation endows this unit with a content which is both emotional and popular. During the age of State wars, the army
was somewhat marginal to the nation: only the nobles could
become officers, while the troops consisted of volunteers or
mercenaries, such as the Swiss regiments. The rest of the
population stayed away from the military life, save whenever
it had to bear the brunt of local campaigns. In those circumstances, it is easy to understand the reason why cabinet politics had been prevalent, and all the military operations
directly subsumed under a framework of negotiations. The two
kinds of action were permanently entwined.The State could at
any time put a stop to the expenditures, as soon as it was
convinced that the game was becoming dangerous. Everything
happened according to rules acknowledged by all the parties
involved, even on the battle-field, where the confrontations
took place in a well-defined order.

The Nation introduced the idea of the people into the
political life taken as a whole. The subject of the State
became citizen, that is to say, full participant in the
political life through suffrage and other means. From this
point of view, the transformation of the State into Nation
revolutionized the very notion of politics. Thus the idea of
equality became the logical substitute of the concept of
class or estate hierarchy. As each member of the Nation is a
citizen on a full and equal basis, at least in principle, it
follows that he is equal before the law, and also before the

military service, so to speak. To be a citizen meant to take part in the political life of the Nation, in all its aspects, and necessarily in its military service. It was the so-called statute of the citizen-soldier. Likewise, in virtue of its internal logic, the Revolution in France made the military service accessible to everybody from February 1790 on. As a result, warfare became everybody's business; said differently, the whole population could be called to arms. Hence it became the people's war. This innovation was in itself revolutionary. It turned tradition upside down: warfare ceased to be a well-regulated undertaking borne by a population that felt unconcerned. Its dynamism fed on popular exaltation and ebullience, and mass movements. It may be remarked in passing that the American War of Independence showed to the young French officers of the time how a people in arms could dispose of the enemy army in the long run by its sheer mass, despite its lack of discipline and its indifference to the established tactical rules and conventions. Later on, the French Revolution would confirm that experience on a larger scale, before an astounded Europe.

As Napoleon's wars would testify, the result was ever bigger armies deployed over ever wider war theatres, and also an increasing ruthlessness in combat. It has often been stressed that political democratization lent a new dimension to warfare by opposing peoples or nations in armed conflicts which with the advent of WWI came to include the whole planet. As a principle of action, democratization cannot be partitioned and contained, because it invades all walks of life, bringing with it its blessings, its perils and its inconveniences. The extension and intensification of warfare were equally favoured by other circumstances, particularly the industrial development and the progress of science and technology. In other words, national wars acquired those familiar dimensions thanks both to an internal dynamism linked to democracy and the idea of equality, and to external conditions, essentialy economic and scientific. It is true, at least as far as the early period is concerned, that the national wars were less frequent than the State wars, as they mobilized all the resources of the nation. In exchange, they were more blood-thirsty and destructive in the intensity of their engagements. Each war would release forces hard to control.

Thus the national war is a genuine about-turn in the relation between warfare and the human being. It is time now to spell out the connections between national wars and revolutionary wars. Without going into much historical detail, I still find it necessary to linger on the innovation introduced by the French Revolution. It was during that period that the link between the national and the revolutionary wars was consolidated.

The battle at Valmy was given in the manner of State wars: the generals of the two opposing camps were manoeuvring according to traditional rules on that occasion. Considering the invasion of French territory sufficient threat, the Duke of Brunswick made his way back to the initial lines. The expedition was proving difficult because of the lingering bad weather and the increasing danger posed by the enveloping manoeuvres on the two flanks, that were led by Dumouriez and Custine, respectively.[33] Besides, as he was pursuing his military operations, Dumouriez was carrying on negotiations. The surprise lay in the enthusiasm with which the French public reacted to the 'victory' at Valmy, reduced as it was to a cannonade, without any troop engagement. In France, general opinion was no longer atuned to the rest of Europe: the national and the revolutionary impetus were at work. The resounding echo of the victory at Jemmapes, several weeks later, only confirms the evolution: the frontal battle was won by the sans-culottes because they overwhelmed the enemy by their sheer number, to the tune of the Carmagnole. The principle of sparing the troops was discarded and instead, making the most of one's numerical superiority in a rabbid attack became the order of the day. The old ways of waging war were becoming obsolete: the large number was prevailing. Besides, the revolutionary was fighting for a cause, what nowadays we call ideology.[34] The weapons were carrying a message. At the same time warfare was becoming ardent and impetuous, because it also meant fighting for ideas.

Ultimately, warfare ceased to be an occupation for mercenaries. The fighter of year II was a patriot and a republican who was defending the soil and his convictions. In his speech of the 12th February, 1793, addressed to the Convention, Saint-Just said clearly: 'You should not expect victory only from numbers and the soldiers' discipline; you will win it thanks to the foray which the republican spirit will make into the army'.[35] Later on, in his address of June 1794 to General Jourdan, Saint-Just added: 'The war of freedom should be waged with fury'.[36] Manoeuvres and negotiations with the enemy were out of the question. The issue was to defeat him completely, even by instant pursuit, if that was necessary. War was becoming an implacable collision that did not spare the generals, either. Thus, Houchard, the victor of Hondschoote, was sentenced and beheaded because he had allowed the English to escape.[37]

A new system of recruitment was made necessary by the expansion of battle-fields and the violence of the engagements. In their turn, both demanded ever more numerous combat effectives to compensate for the high cost in human lives, and cover the vast expanse of the battle-fields. At first, it was 'the mass levy' that was introduced. Typical of the revolutionary period, it made it possible to throw fresh troops into battle without relenting. Later on, that system gave way to a more rational system of conscription. It is quite improbable that without the support of the ideas of Nation and People, conscription would have lasted until the present and spread to almost all the European countries. To bear arms ceased to be a trade carried on by marginal people. It became a public service, instead, that is to say, one aspect of each citizen's civic duty. Conscription brought about the reorganization of the standing army. On the one hand, the military career became a profession with all the inherent specializations characteristic of any well-defined profession, and on the other hand, the contingents of the army could be renewed continuously, with the result that drilling even in time of peace gave each citizen the skill of military techniques. Thus one may talk, at least indirectly, of the people in arms, because in case of need, the greatest number could be called up, on the supposition that everybody had been trained to handle various weapons. As a result, the army came to consist of native citizens almost exclusively.

At the same time, warfare acquired an all-encompassing significance, as it moblilized all the resources of the Nation, people as well as material goods. The stake became enormous. Nobody could evade its burden. As a matter of fact, it ceased to be the exclusive concern of the volunteers of a professional army or of the inhabitants of the region turned into a theatre of operations. One way or another, it came to affect all the citizens of the Nation that could be called up at any time, if need arose. The scant contingents of the State era had nothing in common with the massive armies, made up of millions of men, which the national wars were able to mobilize. Warfare grew more ferocious and murderous, disappointing the expectations of people who, like Chateaubriand, used to think that Napoleon has killed war by exaggerating it'.[38] On the contrary, warfare was drawn into the extreme escalation, mentioned by Clausewitz.[39] It was not a matter of any particular escalation to the extreme, given its objective to break the enemy's resistance, but rather a generalization of the phenomenon. All the subsequent historical evolution of warfare was subjected to this escalatory trend.

The association of the national ideology with the revolutionary ideology brought about a change in the concept of enemy, essential to the understanding of any kind of conflict. Since Richelieu, the State efforts had been aiming at the elimination of the internal enemy, in order to be able to concentrate one's attention upon one enemy only, the external enemy. During the age of State wars, Condé commanded the French and the Spanish armies by turn; Turenne was in the service of the Austrian imperial army and of the French royal army, respectively; although not a French subject, Maurice of Saxe commanded the French army while Eugene of Savoy commanded the Austrian army, though as his name shows, he was not an Austrian. Furthermore, many French officers had their training in the Prussian army. On the other hand, the national wars had their generals recruited exclusively from within the borders of the particular nations, with few exceptions, one of which was Jomini.[40] Eventually, the Nation came to represent the union of the State, the people and the army. Whoever refrained from joining that union became either a suspect, or what is more, a traitor.

The speeches made by the revolutionaries in the aftermath of the war declaration of April 1792 referred both to the internal and the external enemies, in a way that rendered open or cryptic civil wars part of national wars. For a beginning, war was waged against foreign kings, before executing the king of their own country, depicted as a tyrant. The law against suspects of the 17th September, 1793, which introduced the Terror, had as its purpose to pronounce guilty of treason against the Nation everybody who did not adhere

to the official ideology. Robespierre's speech on the 'Principles of Political Morals' is quite explicit on this point:
'The internal and the external enemies of the Republic must
be choked lest we perish with the Republic. In such circumstances, the first rule of your policy must be to lead the
people by the means of reason and the people's enemies by
the means of terror'.[41]

The internal enemy, or presumably so, found his way even
in the very midst of the revolutionaries, as such destinies
as those of a Danton, a Hébert or a Babeuf show.[42] Later on,
the Bolshevik Revolution registered a similar evolution.

The internal enemy assumed some other features, too, as,
for instance, of revolutionary conspirators: the Carbonari
and Garibaldi's Red Shirts are good illustrations.The latter
stirred internal trouble in order to help the external army
in the conquest of national independence. Likewise, it was
a nationalist reflex that stood right behind the revolutionary rising of the Paris Commune of 1871, at the cost of an
extreme confusion regarding the internal and the external
enemies. Here Marx's importance in the matter should not be
overlooked. By his theory of class-struggle, he amplified to
the limit the concept of internal enemy. On the one hand, he
conceived of a universal opposition between the bourgeoisie
and the proletariat, and on the other, he transformed it
into the revolutionary dynamo inside each nation. From
this point of view, Marx was an internationalist revolutionary, but at the same time, he was an ardent German nationalist, too, as many of his writings attest. Here are two
illustrations with reference to the Franco-German War (1870-
1871). Soon after the war declaration, Marx was writing to
Engels that the French needed a thrashing, and added that a
Prussian victory would move the centre of gravity of the
western labour movement from France to Germany, which in turn
would secure the superiority of his and Engels' theory over
Proudhon's.[43] After France's defeat, Engels wrote to Marx:
'First of all, as in 1866, Bismarck has carried out part of
our work, in his own manner and without intending it. ...
Generally speaking, to want to reverse the course of history
because one does not like it, which is Liebknecht's way, is
silly. We know these model Germans of the South quite well.
They are hopeless imbeciles'.[44]

Actually Liebknecht had taken sides against the war,

and his attitude annoyed both Marx and Engels.[45]Likewise,
Marx's well-known 'Russophobia' may equally be explained by
his nationalism.

Social revendications were another reason for the close
connection between the national and the revolutionary wars.
They had already raised their heads during the French Revolution, and grew ever more determined afterwards. The citizen
saw in the military career a kind of promotion, because ad-
vancement to the rank of officer was no longer made conditional on social origin, but rather on personal ability.
The citizen-soldier expected to be rewarded for rendered
services, among other things. In the last instance, it was
a matter of the widest possible application of the equality
principle promoted by the Revolution, and which went beyond
the merely legal or military connotations. The social question formed the background of almost all the national wars,
thus endowing them with a revolutionary factor. In certain
cases, governments, such as Bismarck's, enacted a very
advanced social legislation after the 1870-1871 war, in order
better to combat the revolutionary ideas.

TOTAL WAR AND GUERRILLA WARFARE

An exhaustive analysis of these types of conflict is not
feasible: not only are they still evolving, but also we lack
the necessary distance that would enable us to get a global
image of them both. Nevertheless, books have been written
that try to bring together all available data in order to
facilitate an informed opinion of their evolution. I am
thinking in particular of Raymond Aron's PEACE AND WAR AMONG
NATIONS and CLAUSEWITZ.[46] The interdependence of total war
and guerrilla warfare has nothing logically necessary about
it, although it becomes obvious that guerrilla warfare pro-
liferates at a time when mankind is threatened by total
nuclear war and is already practising total diplomacy.
We are witnessing a quite disconcerting historical correlation: guerrilla warfare is spreading as the most effective
kind of warfare in the shade of the deterrent policy engen-
dered by the thermonuclear arms race. The fear that a nuclear
conflict might turn into an apocalypse, seemingly makes human aggressiveness seek an outlet in the guerrilla warfare

of local wars.

There has been a gap between State wars, with their limited character, on the one hand, and national wars, on the other, despite some common traits, particularly as concerns the standing army. Not the same may be said about the later types of war: a continuity may be easily traced between total and national wars, as well as between revolutionary wars and guerrilla warfare. As shown earlier, by its own nature, the national war was subject to the logic of escalation which could but lead to the idea of total war, regarded as the possible extreme of escalation. Guerrilla warfare, on the other side, came into its own concomittantly with the first genuinely revolutionary war, unleashed by the French Revolution.

National war was carrying the germ of total warfare, so to speak. Unlike the limited State wars that involved only the armies that were formed for that very purpose, the national wars implied the mobilization of the state, the people and the army in the service of the Nation. Indeed, at the beginning, it did not succeed in enlisting all the energies and resources, but the trend was there, at work, as stated in the speeches made by the revolutionaries of 1793. Later, in the aftermath of Napoleon's campaigns, there was a relapse: one tried to subsume national and revolutionary wars to State wars by granting priority to diplomacy. It was the era of balance in politics that started with the negotiations at the Congress of Vienna in 1815. The last act of that diplomacy was the Berlin treaty of 1878 which divided the world among the then world powers, on the basis of diplomatic bargaining. It was also at that time that the first theories of total warfare were put together, more or less as a consequence of the Franco-Prussian war of 1870-1871.

The first significant book on this subject-matter was that by Colmar von der Goltz, THE NATION IN ARMS.[47] One should not mistake total war for Clausewitz's concept of absolute war.[48] The latter means warfare considered in itself, as a universal concept, regardless of the historical, political, economic and social conditions, unlike real war which takes into account those circumstances. Total war is real war that exploits all the circumstances in order to secure victory. It may be said in passing that von der Goltz's work influenced the thinking of later military commanders among whom Foch's. The basic idea was the following: at the start of the war, all the possible conditions must be mustered in order to eliminate the enemy; thus, one must mobilize men and materiel for a decisive battle, which eventually was called the blitzkrieg or lightning war. Nonetheless, even at that time, opinions were divided at the very level of general headquarters. In France, for instance, Foch favoured the idea of a war of annihilation, relying on a decisive victory scored at the beginning of the operations. On the other hand, Joffre refused to stake everything on a battle, thinking that it was necessary to portion out one's efforts in time, in order to be capable of delivering other battles, were the first lost.[49] In Germany, the problem was marked by the debate between the elder Moltke and Schlieffen, while the younger Moltke supported Schlieffen's theses.[50] In his last speech delivered before the Reichstag in May 1890, the elder Moltke stated that the new kind of war ran the risk of being bogged, and as a result, it was necessary to prepare for a series of confrontations in order to prevail over the opponent by wearing him out. Schlieffen, on the other hand, thought that by its huge expenditures of men and materiel, the new kind of war could not be reconciled with the needs of modern trade and industry, and for that reason, its pace ought to be rapid so as to reach a resolution from the first engagements.[51] He was reasoning essentially in the terms of absolute warfare as coined by Clausewitz. The result is known.

By consistently reserving all available capabilities for the combat, Schlieffen rendered himself guilty of the error of conceiving warfare exclusively in the terms of plain, strategical planning, without sufficiently taking into consideration the political conditions of the period. It was a politician, Walter Rathenau, who at the beginning of WWI tried to fill in the blanks in Schlieffen's plans, preparing Germany for a long war through his policy for a war economy. Notwithstanding, the concept of total war was perfected only after WWI, following Ludendorff's prolonged, retrospective meditation upon Germany's defeat. Once more it was the vanquished who drew the lesson from the events. Ludendorff put his thoughts into a book, published in 1922, under the title, KRIEGFÜHRUNG UND POLITIK, and then, in 1935, into another, DER TOTALE KRIEG.[52] I shall not insist on his subordination of politics to military action, but rather on his idea that war was no longer limited to the front as it demanded the mobilization of all the resources, whether economic, diplomatic, moral, journalistic, and so on. In other words, war is won in factories, editorial offices, propaganda bureaux and intelligence services, as well. Thus, in the terms of the idea of total war as envisaged by Ludendorff, it was not enough to destroy the enemy's military capability; it was also necessary to act upon the civilian population, in order to break its moral resistance, even at the cost of spreading panic behind the lines by massive bombing. Treated as recommendations and not as mere aspects of a theoretical concept, they were put to practical use by both camps during WWII.

The thermonuclear war risks to overreach total war in horror and catastrophe. The destructive capabilities are such that they may make havoc of the prudence of politics, were the latter ever to resort to such weapons. It is true that according to the principle of deterrence, we have entered the extreme phase of the accumulation of nuclear weapons, rather than that of their use. Said differently, one piles up quantities of weapons, by far larger than one anticipates to be obliged to make actual use of. Enemies are no longer threatened on the battle-field, but much earlier, during and by the preparations for a war which they claim that they do not want to wage. It is the so-called peaceful coexistence which is, as Raymond Aron stressed, a kind of stabilization by mutual fear of the apocalyptic effects of a subsequent nuclear war. Nonetheless, the so-called conventional weapons keep piling up and are continuously perfected. Considering the speed of the technological progress, such weapons are likely to become obsolete within a decade or two of their manufacture. The temptation to use those weapons is great whenever the balance of forces is perceived as favourable, in order to avoid being overburdened by the heavy economic expenses demanded by the incessant technical innovations. These questions elude both ethnology and sociology. Even the most sophisticated futurology is unable to choose among the various possible hypotheses, because the unleashing of a war depends on human will and not on the findings of scientific inquiry.

Stated in Delbrück's categorical terms, total war corresponds problematically to the strategy of annihiliation. Nevertheless, in the field, it is accompanied by a strategy of attrition, to everybody's surprise. Practically, the latter assumes the form of guerrilla warfare, which seems to proliferate in the shade of the deterrence effected by nuclear terror, and allows the revolutionary ideology to expand under the cover of nationalism or self-determination. Indeed, there have always been irregular fighters throughout history, such as Aristonicos' companions fighting to recover the kingdom of Pergamus from the Romans,[53] the peasant wars of the Middle Ages, the followers of Fra Dolcino, or finally, the Calvinists in the Cévennes opposing resistance to Louis XIV's army. The modern type of partisan made his appearance during the French Revolution, yet not to defend it, but rather to fight it. Mention should be made of the rising of the Vendée, Jean Chouan's insurgents in the West of the country, the various revolts against Napoleon abroad, as in Spain or in Tyrol, where the followers of Hofer and Haspringer took the initiative. It was at that time that one came to grasp the impact which that kind of warfare could have. At any rate, Napoleon took it seriously when in 1813 he told General Lefebvre that one should act as a partisan wherever there were partisans.[54] The king of Prussia, head of a legitimate State, even went so far as to sign a decree in April 1813, by which he rendered lawful the organization of guerrilla warfare, though the decree was never implemented. Likewise, Clausewitz is known to have appreciated the importance of the phenomenon.[55] Later on, one comes across the incursions undertaken by Garibaldi's Red Shirts and the operations carried out by the French sharp shooters against the Germans in 1871, after Gambetta had declared 'war without restraint', appealing in this way to national and popular feelings.

Nevertheless, it is Lenin who may be considered the main theoretician of the typical revolutionary partisan. The outline is inserted in his description of the professional revolutionary in his WHAT IS TO BE DONE? of 1901,[56] to which it should be added an article of 1906 on partisan warfare, as well as his notes on Cluseret, the military commander of the Paris Commune and author of a book on street fighting, that foreshadows the present-day urban guerrilla warfare. The formula found its massive application in the countries occupied by Nazi Germany, in China and in Cuba (with further theoretical contributions by Mao and Che Guevara),[57] as well as in Indochina and Algeria. Today's terrorist movements

derive from the same source, though the influence exerted
upon them by the anarchists of the turn of the century, such
as Nechaev and Tkachev need not be dismissed. After all,
Lenin had read their books, but opposed individual terrorism
in favour of collective terrorism. What are the characteristic features of this kind of warfare?

Often enough, guerrilla warfare has been given the name of
'little war'. That made a lot of sense in the past, but
decreasingly so since, owing to its generalization and to the
fact that very quickly after its precarious start, it could
make the most of the modern means of communication and
sophisticated weapons, sometimes especially manufactured for
it. As a matter of fact, and generally speaking, guerrilla
warfare, which in its early days made use of irregular
fighters, has eventually developed into a type of war waged
by regular troops. This evolution implies a play of forces
on two planes: an irregular and a regular. As long as it remains confined to guerrilla warfare, the fighting is characterized by the great mobility of a small number of effective
combatants, surprise attacks, feints and resilience both in
attack and in retreat. This latter feature has been repeatedly insisted upon by various theoreticians interested in
this kind of conflict. [58] There are nonetheless some other
features that to me seem even more typical, nay, basic.

First of all, guerrilla warfare which is conditioned by
terrain may reach extreme intensity in the way it uses
harrassment. As things are, it is localized because it depends on the complicity of the local population. It is
hard to imagine partisan warfare developing in the midst of
an alien population. Che Guevara paid with his life this
oversight. The Vietcong partisans were active within the
boundaries of Vietnam, and the fellagha within the Algerian
borders. The Vietnamese crossed their borders only after they
managed to put together a regular army of their own. A
partisan war waged by Vietnamese in the Philippines or in
Australia is hard to think of; and even harder it is to
imagine a general, world-wide, partisan war. Within its con-
fines, however, partisan warfare is total, because it resorts
to every available means, those of terrorism and hostage-
taking, and others, such as the hold-up, equally spectacular,
meant to impress the population. Such acts throw the ordinary
process of justice into confusion, because the latter can

differentiate only between criminal and political violence. By its intensity, partisan warfare is total warfare even when it is limited to a slow manouevre of attrition against the enemy because, as Guy Doly remarks, its objective is to convince the adversary to give up fighting.[59] Haste is not needed to reach that objective. The resistance opposed is long-lasting, on condition that a third, regular party is found willing to assure its representativeness. Harrassment on the part of the guerrilla, on the other hand, is extreme by necessity, given the asymmetry of the forces involved on both sides, and the political stake. The Americans engaged only part of their forces in Vietnam, whereas the Vietcong were each time forced to throw all their effectives into the war, under the impression that they were fighting for their lives. A similar difference in attitude obtains between the Palestinians and the other Arab nations.

Secondly, guerrilla warfare is essentially tactical, placed in the service of a political strategy defined by national and revolutionary ideologies. It was Giap who said that political work is the soul of the army.[60] The soldier of a regular army fulfills a civic duty, whereas the partisan of an irregular army is a volunteer who has made a clear and definite political choice, and who as a result, is led to utilize every means in order to secure the victory of his cause. That is why propaganda, as a psychological weapon, is as important as the machine-gun or the bomb. In this particular case, propaganda enjoys the advantage of the mystique of secrecy, above all whenever it is accompanied by surprise and spectacular assassination attempts. All the subversive methods are good. The direct confrontation sought by the enemy should be avoided as long as possible, because victory in partisan warfare is the fruit of the accumulation of small successes that demoralize the enemy but reassure the population whose spokesman the partisans are, according to Mao's slogan, 'let us fight to win the masses'.[61]

Total warfare and the revolutionary guerrilla warfare have had a decisive effect upon the classical system of international relations and upon the idea of peace. They simply dismembered the system observed by the national and the revolutionary wars, although, truth to say, they are not alone responsible for the demolition: the watershed, which so many declarations of independence brought about after WWII, could but call in question the system of European Civil Law which the Western world had so painfully worked out since the Renaissance.[62] In the world forum, as well as inside the various international organizations, the European countries are in minority. It was to be expected that the non-Europeans would make havoc of the classical international law, without for that matter being able to produce a replacement system, so far. The proliferation of terrorist acts, the highjacking of airplanes, the taking of hostages, all prove the deterioration of the principles worked out by the Westerners, and at times with their connivance. Even the very idea of a peace treaty is called in question. According to the classical system, every war was concluded by a peace treaty which incorporated the results of negotiations between the victor and the defeated, and the treaty in turn became a document of international relations. The Treaty of Versailles of 1918 put an end to that tradition, because the negotiations took place among the allies only and the treaty as such was imposed upon the defeated. After WWII there was not even a peace treaty with the main defeated party, namely Germany, a fact which could only further destabilize the international relations.[63]

It is impossible to foresee the new international regulations because of the very prestige enjoyed in the ideological sphere by the revolutionary guerrilla warfare, that warfare waged by irregular fighters. Seemingly a strange, mental process is at work that makes people give priority to irregularity in social matters over the regularity of the law.

Furthermore, the speed with which technical innovations are introduced in the production of weapons obstructs the establishment of new conventions. How is it possible to work out new agreements among countries when the incessant technological advance keeps disrupting the principles of an agreement? An international conference has sense only if it is summoned to regulate lasting relations among nations. The continuous flow of technological innnovations in the military sphere makes short shrift of the indispensable time duration which negotiated agreements need in order to be carried into effect.

IV

EVOLVING TECHNICAL ASPECTS OF WARFARE

It goes without saying that the available weapons have each and every time determined the character of the war waged or to be waged, its destructive capability and the deployment of the troops summoned to battle. Even the ways in which surprise and retreat are made use of have been altered by the weapons at hand. Unfortunately, this aspect of the problem has been paid little attention, and few are the books, as a result, which establish a relationship between the conduct of the combatants and the weapons with which they are equipped. One of these books is the already-mentioned pioneer work of Johannes Ullrich, THE WAR THROUGHOUT THE AGES. Without going into detail about its contents, three points of the complex relationship, which it deals with, need to be singled out, however briefly: 1. the technological evolution of weaponry; 2. the system of combat troop deployment, and 3. the art of commanding.[1]

Nonetheless, before embarking upon their analysis, stress should be laid upon the turnabout operated by mechanization, because it altered the relation between man and warfare thoroughly. The change did not pass unnoticed by contemporaries, however. Thus, for instance, visiting the battlefield at Eylau after the battle, Napoleon is said to have exclaimed: 'What butchery!' Other people witnessed it with mixed feelings of fear and nostalgia, regretting the wars of the past that had been as many occasions to put to the test the soldier's physical and moral qualities, his endurance and his sense of honour. From then on, it was the trajectory of an impersonal bullet or of a shell that decided the issue of a battle. Personal courage has taken a back seat, daring and heroism have become obsolete, because what counts now is the range of the mechanical weapons. The relative moderation of previous wars gives in to the human masses and the great number of machines. Joseph de Maistre was one of the most eloquent analysts of the phenomenon, as shown by the description he gave in the seventh dialogue of his book, ST. PETERSBURG: 'No nation was victorious at the expense of another nation. ... Mutual concern, the most refined politeness knew how to make themselves manifest amidst the din of arms. The cannon ball in the air avoided the royal palace, many a time, dances and theatre performances were interludes to battle. The enemy officer invited to those festivities would come and talk laughingly of the battle of the following day; and even amidst the horror of the bloodiest skirmishes, the dying could still hear the accents of pity and the formulas of courtesy in the voices around him'. [2]

Mechanical innovations combined with the enrollment of the citizen-soldiers expanded the ranks of the army that threw ever larger numbers into battles, which as a result, were growing ever bloodier. Suffices to remember that the five years of WWII registered more casualties than all the forces in men and weapons mustered by the armies of the seventeenth and the eighteenth centuries, taken together. Roger Caillois is correct when he points out a direct relationship between the birth of modern democracies and the expansion and intensity of warfare. [3]

TECHNOLOGICAL EVOLUTION OF WEAPONRY AND
THE ORGANIZATION OF TROOP DEPLOYMENT

This subject-matter can be dealt with only in general terms here, on the basis of several examples taken from history. The phalanx was the Greeks' tactical unit: it was made up of infantrymen, the hoplites, who manoeuvred in compact formations of several ranks. The cavalry was but an auxiliary force. The primacy enjoyed by the footmen can be explained by the fact that the hoplite was a citizen who as such was defending his land, his city, his freedom, unlike the Persians who had an important cavalry, made up of professional soldiers. The hoplite's essential weapons were his spear and his shield, his helmet and his corslet. He also carried a short sword, and wore greaves to protect his legs. The superiority of the Greek phalanx lay in the fact that in battle, the fighters in the last rank could fill the gaps in the first line at speed. Nevertheless, such a formation also had its weaknesses. It had vulnerable flanks and was unable to pursue the routed enemy. The Greek tactic was essentially a tactic of attrition and not of annihilation. Bearing in mind the fact that the hoplite was a free citizen, it is easy to understand why the warrior's main virtues were of a moral order, as Xenophon never failed to stress: individual stamina, self-confidence and determination, but he lacked the manoeuvring skills that were acquired during protracted drills. Thus it is understandable also why it was considered an honour to engage in battle in the first rank.[4] The first, significant innovation was Epaminondas' deployment of troops in an oblique order, meant to reduce the vulnerability of the flanks.[5] Nonetheless, it was Philip II of Macedonia and Alexander the Great who brought about a radical change by adding the cavalry unit to the phalanx. As a consequence, annihilation got the edge over attrition in warfare, because the horsemen were able to pursue the defeated enemy. At the same time, the way was opened for a professional army, essentially made up of mercenaries.[6] The citizen-soldier ceased to exist as the Greek polis was losing its political status. With the appearance of the diadochs, the city-states were speedily turning into mere, provincial towns within larger administrative units.[7]

The Roman legion went through a similar evolution, although Marius created the cohort, a tactical unit smaller than the legion. Two other elements in the evolution of the legion are worth remembering. At a certain moment, the Romans and the natives of the Italian peninsula found it beyond their abilities to control the conquests of the Empire. As a result, it became necessary to resort to mercenary barbarians: Germans, Heruli, Moors, Syrians, Arabs and the like, who ended by deposing the Roman emperors and imposing their own chiefs. Secondly, the cavalry gradually outweighed the disciplined legionary infantry which had been the strength of the phalanx and of the legion. Belisarius and Narses, Emperor Justinian's generals, were essentially commanders of cavalry formations.[8] That evolution was not solely due to an internal cause. It should be remembered that the peoples that were threatening the boundaries of the Empire had their own hordes of horsemen. It was vital to adapt to the new kind of warfare waged by the Goths, the Huns, and later on, by the Arabs and the Mongols. The new type of army was capable of covering a huge space quickly, without however, being able to control it politically. The civilization of footmen was succeeded by a civilization of horsemen, the knights.

The medieval cavalry had a particular system of fortifications as the base for its development. Widukind, a tenth-century historian, explains the process in his DEEDS OF THE SAXONS.[9] The Germanic king Henry the Fowler ordered the erection of military stations, called burg, and meant to defend the local population against the incursions of the Hungarian horsemen. Each burg was placed in the charge of a commander whose job was to maintain the defences, organize the resistance, build barns to store the harvests and save them from pillage. The local population compensated the man in charge by contributions in kind, given the fact that his tasks prevented him from participating in any of the ordinary occupations. This military organization, which in the long run was extended to the whole of Europe against such invaders as the Arabs, Normen or the Tartars, contributed to the development of a particular political structure. The office of the commander of the burg became hereditary, in virtue of an established custom.[10] Thus a military invention came to influence the political organization. Each holder of a fief acquired a relative autonomy within the vassalage system with its consecrations and honour code. The fief-holder maintained his own more or less important retinue of armed men. For various reasons, they would fight each other, firstly in private wars, and later on, in tournaments. Indeed, in principle at least, the army still kept fulfilling its protective role, but grew marginal in its relationship with the population, which unlike the citizen-soldiers of antiquity, did not join in the military life, with few and far-between exceptions among the infantrymen, such as the symptomatic units of archers and pikers. The military profession had become the occupation of a caste. The battles were reduced to a series of individual combats on horseback. Consistent with the image of the anarchical organization of the medieval society, the troops ignored any discipline, which also meant any integration within a collective unit. There was simply no tactical unit such as the phalanx or the legion of earlier times. Everything was made dependent upon the impetuosity of the adversaries. Likewise, with the exception of one or two great battles, most of the encounters were mere skirmishes, in which the first blow designated the victor. In fact, the knight's equipment and that of his horse had grown heavier with time, making it impossible to manoeuvre for lack of mobility.

As early as the thirteenth century, the system began to decline, concurrently with the urban revival and the appearance of a bourgeois, commercial patriciate. In order to survive, the fief-holders would sell or mortgage their estates. The cities had their own armies which at the beginning were autochthonous militias, but gradually turned into mercenary armies, and so the knights in their turn began to offer themselves for hire to the new power-holders in the cities. The invention of the fire-arm and of the artillery rendered fortresses increasingly vulnerable. A new civilization of infantrymen was on its way with the advent of the Renaissance, and of which Machiavelli was one of the early theoreticians. The cavalry, which previously had been called 'the ordinary of war',[11] did not disappear altogether. It was transformed thoroughly on the pattern of a tactical unit, namely the squadron, with a certain degree of discipline and integration, comparable to those of the infantry. By the way, the term 'infantry' dates from the sixteenth century.[12] Simultaneously, another fighting service became increasingly important as a consequence of the discovery of overseas territories: the navy.

The earliest form of the new infantry was that of the halberdiers of Swiss and Flemish origin. It was a collective formation, divided into fanions, capable of carrying out autonomous manoeuvres. It was simultaneously with this new troop formation that titles such as colonel, adjutant, sergeant, and so on, made their appearance. One after another, different countries adopted the new formula with contingent variations, as shown by the French and the Spanish infantry during the Italian wars. Once more the cavalry came to serve as support force, though this time, in concert with the artillery, the evolution of which is short of the miraculous. The different kinds of wars originating in the turmoils characteristic of the Renaissance and which had already been mentioned, whether they were State, national, revolutionary or guerrilla wars, but not total wars, gave priority to the infantry. We shall return to them only to underline the technological innovations and the organization of the troops.

The new preponderance of the infantry returned the primacy to the tactical unit, which in the process also gained in resilience and acquired a logical instrumentality, superior to that of the Greek phalanx or the Roman legion. I shall not

linger upon the incipient forms of the new kind of deployment in the theatre of operations, such as the Spanish
tercio,or the flat formations of the Dutch or Orange armies.
What needs to be insisted upon here is the new organization
of the infantry which had the company for its base, and a new
hierarchy based on number: the batallion, the regiment, the
brigade, the division, and so on. The other fighting services
copied the tactical unit formula of the infantry, and so the
cavalry, the navy and even the air force would get their
squadrons while the artillery, its battery. More recently,
other tactical units even more mobile have seen the light of
day, showing a increased capacity to respond to instant decisions, such as the commandos.[13] The latter bring together
the fire power of a light artillery, the participation of
aircraft, the manoeuvres of the infantry and the methods of
guerrilla warfare. The aircraft carriers are the equivalent
of the commandos at sea. What is worth noting here is that
the tactical units tend to evolve towards an increasingly
precise rationalization of tactics within the military organization. We shall come back to it later on, in our analysis
of strategy.

In the case of the infantry,the technical innovations con-
centrated by and large upon the weapons in use. For a start,
the musketeers replaced the pikers; then, the discovery of
the spiralling fire led to alternate ranks of shooters in
shooting position and of those who were reloading their fire-
arms, respectively. The bayonet united the piker and the
musketeer into one and the same individual person while com-
bining the white weapon with the fire-arm. Later on, a more
rational regrouping of the infantry fire was achieved by in-
troducing the principle of the salvo, and even more so, that
of the platoon. Afterwards, the automatic firing gun was
invented, with such perfected variants as the heavy machine-
gun and the tommy gun. These invetions, however, did not affect the tactical unity of the infantry,but only its deployment as companies of shooters and then of fusiliers were added, the latter being flanked at first by the light infantrymen, endowed with greater mobility because they did not fight
in keeping with the rules of the compact formation of the
'square' which had been in use for some time. Despite the
fact that it was continuously equipped with new weapons, such
as the mine-launcher, the grenade and the flame-thrower, the

infantry gradually came to occupy a secondary place, as a new cavalry formation made its appearance: the mechanized cavalry.

During the renewed preeminence of the infantry, the changes in warfare were marked by the development of the artillery. Strangely enough, though, in the seventeenth century, the latter showed its worth not in foot combat, but in naval engagements and in the defensive systems of fortifications. Actually, since the ancient times, the artillery had a role to play with its catapults and rams, which gradually gave way to the various kinds of ballistae, such as the mangonel and the bombard. Thus, it was only indirectly that the cannon came to make an impact upon the infantry and its super-structure. Richelieu's policy of natural borders found its military solution in Vauban's system of fortifications. In order to ensure the safety of the State, Vauban transformed old fortresses and ordered the construction of new ones. His system of fortifications integrated the capabilities of the artillery of the time, its cross-fire and ricochet fire. The artillery became a much dreaded arm at sea, because of the long range of its fire. As a consequence, both the privateers and the pirates used it to their profit.

It is owing to the Swedish king Gustavus Adolphus that the infantry and the artillery were first combined rationally on a trial basis. He equipped his infantrymen with lighter can-nons that had a greater firing range. Gribeauval's action [14] was as decisive, because thanks to him, the artillery was raised to the status of a new, autonomous service branch. Napoleon turned to account Gribeauval's insights through the massive concetration of the artillery upon the points which he considered decisive for the next battle, in his prep-arations of the offensive of his infantry. Besides, Napoleon was the first strategist to reason in terms of masses, never tiring to repeat that he never had enough troops or enough weapons. That approach is still decisive in our times, despite the fact that many improvements of a technological order have been accumulating.

The most effective technological innovations that changed the way wars are waged, however, were made during WWI, with the appearance of a new weapon: the airplane, a more manage-able tool for the control of the skies than the aerostat. In no time, the air force was made to fulfill two basic tasks: surveillance and combat. A reconnaissance air force was escorted and protected by fighter planes, equipped with machine guns for combat. The planes could also carry bombs meant for the destruction of various objectives behind the front lines. The second important innovation was the tank, which excelled in breaching enemy positions. At the same time, the role of the classical cavalry was shrinking accordingly, so practically, by the end of WWI, it came to be used in transportation where it was challenged by the railway and the motor truck. Furthermore, older technological innovations were exploited extensively as, for instance, in the field of communications, to say nothing of the submarine and the use it was put to. Indeed, warfare was assuming new looks.

All those novelties were fully exploited during WWII, and particularly the aircraft in combination with the tank. That also led to a change in combat: the positional war was replaced by the mobile war of incursion and disruption. The trench combat of WWI had immobilized the two opposing infantries, facing each other in ceaseless manoeuvres of attrition. That was also the last instance of the supremacy of the infantry in modern warfare. As a matter of fact, during WWII, the annihilation strategy won the upper hand by the joint action of the tank and the aircraft. The great battles were fought by the mechanized troops both in 1940, and later, in the Russian plains and in Normandy. The infantry had virtually no other function but that of occupying the territory conquered by the new kind of cavalry. The exceptions were the commando operations and the guerrilla warfare.

A new civilization of the mechanized cavalry was being fostered when a new weapon, with unimaginably destructive effects, appeared at the end of the war: the atomic bomb. The evolution process is going on, but its direction and consequences elude the sociologist.

THE ART OF COMMANDING

Technological development and its implicit specialization in the military sector did not leave the commander's ways unaffected. In yonder times, the political leader and the war chief were generally one and the same person. Leonidas, for instance, was king of Sparta and the army commander at Thermopylae.[15] It was the same in the case of Alexander the

Great and the Persian kings. Likewise, the Roman consul
was both a political and a military leader. Philip Augustus
filled both offices simultaneously, as would do Francis I,
Charles XII of Sweden, Frederick II of Prussia or Napoleon,
later on. There were exceptions, notwithstanding. Although,
in principle, Louis XIV was the chief of his armies,he would
charge·Condé, Turenne or Villars with the command of the military operations, and so did the Austrian emperor who en-
trusted Eugene of Savoy with the military command. The
theoretical distinction between the politicians and the
military is relatively recent. Although empirically it was
already signalled in the writings of Machiavelli and Hobbes,
it was Clausewitz that expounded it theoretically. At this
point, however, it seems to me more important to examine the
two notions of tactics and strategy, instead. Nowadays
they are fully characteristic of any military commander's
decisions.

Indeed, the two notions are of Greek origin,but at present
they mean something different from what they used to, in antiquity. In Athens, the strategus was the magistrate in
charge of military affairs, and there were ten of these
magistrates, one for each deme. Notwithstanding, they did not
automatically assume the command during a real war. When
Xenophon talked about tactics, he meant military drill,
rather than the manouevres on a battle-field.[16]At Rome, the
word strategus designated the authority which went with any
office, whether it was that of a consul, a pretor, a provincial governor, or of the person presiding over a banquet.
Even more strangely, the term 'tactics' is virtually absent
from the surviving written evidence,although the Romans were
masters of tactics. It should be remembered that in ancient
times, warfare was basically tactical and not strategic, in
the modern sense of the word. The tactical units, which were
the phalanx, the legion and the cohort, were manoeuvred with
the greatest possible ability. Some exceptional minds had
some inkling of strategy as we understand it nowadays. One
of them was Alcibiades with his plan for an expedition to
Sicily,[17]yet Julius Caesar, who seems to have followed some
kind of overall plan in his campaigns, plausibly surpasses
them all. Given his personal qualities as sacerdos, he
was a general who knew how to exploit the prestige he had
gained by the conquest of Gaul. He was a risk-taking ma-

noeuvrer and a skilled politician and manipulator who, for
instance, ordered the display of a kind of wall gazette in
the forum, to keep the Roman citizens informed about current
events. One thing is certain, though, namely that the Roman
conquests had not been the result of a preconceived plan, but
of a succession of happy enterprises that expanded through
the prompt exploitation of the advantages scored on the
battle-field, backed by an admirable talent for organization.

With few exceptions, among them Henry the Fowler, the
Middle Ages ignored not only strategy but also the principles of tactics, in the absence of any tactical unit. Indeed, chivalry had its rites, but its military capacity was
limited to surprise attacks carried out with speed and often
followed by plunder. It lacked an overall view even of the
battle-field. The reactions to the incidents in progress were
often blind and disorderly, left to the chance of circumstances. Military thinking took some time to be associated
once more with policy or a political programme, which in the
case of Machiavelli, was the unification of Italy. To that
end he was advocating the creation of a national militia,
free of the flaws displayed by the Swiss and Spanish infantries that would have withstood the French cavalry. What was
needed was a change of tactics. In Machiavelli's opinion,
it would lend prestige to a new prince and render his rule
illustrious.[19] His rational, political thinking implied a correlation between military action and diplomatic negotiation,
between the defence policy and the foreign policy. By start-
ing from the principle that one needs to prepare for war in
time of peace, he went on to integrate the diplomatic action
into the overall strategic plan of the head of State.

Among the earliest reflections on the military phenomenon
in the modern sense of the word, were those of Furet who,
in 1690, defined tactics as the science of deploying the
soldiers in battle formation, and of military evolutions. [20]
Concurrently, a new era of military writings saw the light of
day. It counted among its contributors the like of Feuquière,
Folard, Lloyd, [21] Marshal of Saxe and king Frederick II of
Prussia, alongside Guibert who, as already said, was the
first to work out a comprehensive theory of the art of war.
Later on, reflecting on Napoleon's wars, which they had come
to experience on both sides, Georges de Chambray and Jomini
would publish their own treatises on the art of war. [22] The

latter started from the following premise: there is a small
number of fundamental principles of warfare which one cannot
ignore without incurring danger, and the practical application of which has almost always been crowned by success. ...
Of all the theories of the art of war, the only reasonable
one is that which is grounded in the study of military history, admits certain regulatory principles, but in rest,
leaves most of the general conduct of war to natural genius,
without constraining it by exclusive rules.[23]

With that in view, Jomini went on to draw a distinction
between war policy, on the one hand, and military policy,on
the other: the former establishes the political objectives
which a State adopts while at war, whereas the latter refers
to the military means which the State resorts to in order to
attain the political objectives. In this way, the difference
between political decision and military command was outlined.
It was the military commander's task to work out a strategy
and to prepare the tactics.[24]

Nevertheless, Clausewitz was the one to formulate the new
doctrine most satisfactorily, in his book ON WAR. Two points
in it are essential to the question dealt with in this chap-
ter.The first is the subordination of the military action to
the political action, which implies the distinction between
policy and military directive. Let us recall the already-
quoted formula: 'War is but the continuation of policy by
other means'. Hence war is but one of the instruments available in the practice of politics. Obviously there is nothing
to prevent a military officer from becoming a political
leader, or the other way round. Still, in either of these
cases, it is incumbent on the military officer to wage the
war solely within the framework of the objectives willed by
the politician. Thus the ancient confusion between the head
of State and the head of the army is dispelled. The head of
State does not need to be familiar with the production process and the use of various weapons. His business, so to
speak, is to take the political decision to make or not to
make war. Although in a different garb, the rational law of
the division of labour is easily recognizable here. There is
also a distinction between ends, which need not be overlooked: the end which the military commander pursues is
victory, whereas the ultimate end of the politician is to
set up and consolidate the subsequent peace.

The second point concerns the distinction between strategy and tactics. It is in a short work of 1804, entitled STRATEGIE and which remained unpublished for a long time, that Clausewitz gave the clearest definition of the two concepts: 'Tactics teach us how to secure victory by using the armed forces in combat. Strategy, on the other hand, shows us how to attain the war objective by a combination of operations. To put it in more ellegant terms: tactics teach the utilization of the armed forces in combat, while strategy teaches the use of battles in the interest of the ultimate objective of the war'.[25]

In the last instance, tactics consist of all the manoeuvres on the battle-field, that depend on the abilities of the commanders on the spot and whose concerted actions aim at victory through the destruction of the enemy's moral and material resources. Thus tactics are exclusively at the service of warfare, free of any interference on the part of politics. Strategy, on the other hand, is dependent on the interests of politics and on its goals in the case of each particular war. It is incumbent on the strategist to work out the plan, or plans, of war by taking into consideration the different potential enemies and the variety of political objectives, whether one goes to war against a certain enemy or another. Furthermore, he has to take into account the available military equipment, the moral resources involved in the war effort, both of the military and of the civilian population, as well as of the enemy himself. It is also his task to think out the element of surprise from the start, which plays a decisive part in the conclusion of the war. The strategist works with hypotheses and simulations the aim of which is to reduce the uncertainties of war as much as possible. Finally, once the war is started, strategy is expected to coordinate the various tactical manoeuvres that are performed in the field.

The increasing role played by strategy in modern warfare has several consequences, of which two seem to me to be of capital importance: the first is the establishment of permanent strategical head-quarters, the task of which is to modify the plans of the potential operations in keeping with the country's political developments and the evolution of international relations, as well as with the innovations and other changes that occur in the manufacture of weapons. The second consequence is the redudancy of the supreme military commander's presence on the battle-field, in the image of a Napoleon at Arcole or at Austerlitz. Nowadays he works on maps and blue prints, often far away from the battle-field, and at times, in the safety of a bunker. His skill as war commander rests in the efficiency with which he orders the manoeuvres and coordinates them, and no longer as in yonder times, in his exemplary conduct, his personal courage and enterprising spirit in the field, in the midst of his troops.

After Clausewitz, the works on war strategy multiplied beyond expectations. Some of their authors would claim discipleship, more or less accurately, among them Schlieffen and Foch, while others, following in Ludendorff's footsteps, would think his ideas obsolete and turn his famous formula upside down: global politics must be placed in the service of war. Nevertheless, Clausewitz's ideas were upheld by the head-quarters of standing armies and influenced the orientation of the revolutionary parties, as rendered evident both by Lenin's and Mao's statements. The wide range of interpretations, the object of which it was in the world of politics, points to the rich substance of ON WAR, although strategic thinking also developed outside its framework. The latter either rejected it altogether, as in the case of Liddell-Hart, or ignored it, as happened with Cluseret, the general of the Paris Commune and author of a pioneering book on street battle, who was interested in other aspects of warfare.[26] More recently, other theoreticians, ·the so-called neo-Clausewitzians, among them Raymond Aron, have tried to formulate the questions of a possible nuclear war within the guidelines provided by Clausewitz's strategical conceptualization.[27] Whatever the reactions, one thing is certain: Clausewitz's military writings have deeply marked military thinking for almost two hundred years, and would continue to do so, even if contested.

For almost a century now, there has been an abundance of scientific and pseudo-scientific writings on warfare and the military. As already said, the actual conduct of war is an art and not a science, because it implies action and decision. Nonetheless, strategy has made increasing use of theoretical analyses not only in matters of equipment, but also of human political conduct in times of war and in times of peace.

Among the earliest were the geopolitical studies. It was a

a Swede, Kjellen, who coined the word 'geopolitics', though
the analyses which he associated with it had preceded it.
I have in mind in particular those of Ratzel, a German,
Mackinder, a Briton, and Vidal de la Blanche.[28] Geopolitics
concentrates upon the geographical space. Its aim is to as-
sert the extent to which political relations can be determined
with reference to strategical and diplomatic capabilities,
given a country's geographical situation (continental or mar-
itime) and its economic resources. Geostrategy is a more
recent branch of knowledge which attempts to integrate the
findings of geopolitics into the practical projects of strategy.[29] Another direction is that assumed by polemology and
peace research with their many think-tanks. Their scope is
more comprehensive than that of geopolitics. In the case of
polemology, for instance, the object of study is conflict,
under all its aspects: military, demographic, religious,
ethnological, legal, economic, technological, ideological,
and what have you. Likewise, it does not refrain from the
study of the various characteristic features of the bellicose
act, such as biological aggression, the manifestation of the
sacred, the festive enactment, the sense of sacrifice or the
fascination exerted by fighting.[30] The difference between the
peace-research institutes and the institutes for the study
of conflict is by and large a matter of principle and orientation: being pacifist, the former are partial to the analysis of peace as a phenomenon, while polemology, claiming to
be more scientific, thinks that in order to understand peace,
one must first of all grasp the phenomenon of war. Still
more recently, increased specialization brought to the fore
other branches of research, such as the sociology of war and
the military, ethology, and so on.

On the other hand, it is worth noting that despite the manifest peace-loving orientation in our times, military life
and strategic organization exert their own influence upon the
minds of our contemporaries and upon non-military activities:
they are treated as models. It is a sociological fact, and a
capital one for that matter, which the experts in the field
tend to overlook for reasons that seem to be more ideological
than scientific. Let us take two examples only, in order to
illustrate the point. Either capitalist or socialist, economy
places itself under the sign of strategy and military categories. As a matter of fact, the economies of the socialist

countries would openly claim that their origins go back to the war economy, devised by Walter Rathenau, under the pretext of their continuous exposure to a perpetual aggression on the part of their capitalist competitors. Furthermore, the very idea of planning is conceived in strategic terms, in such a manner that its vocabulary is essentially military: conquest, rebound, mobilization of resources, economic espionage, and so on. It all happens as if peace is only provisional and that given favourable circumstances, the assault would be launched upon the rival economic system. [31] The economy of the so-called democratic nations also resorts to the principle of strategy, though in a different sense. [32] On the other hand, political parties are attuned to military organization either in the way of para-military formations, as were the SA and the SS, or by drilling women and children in the use of arms. Once more Lenin took the initiative when he wrote about his party's structure in WHAT IS TO BE DONE?: 'What we need is a military organization of agents'. [33] Actually, the whole chapter entitled 'What Type of Organization Do We Require?' refers repeatedly to military strategy, even in the preparation of the revolution. The latter was not to be the result of a spontaneous mass explosion, but an attack, an assault launched by a standing formation. The triumphant revolution has but followed the trace marked by the military organization. Besides these two examples from the spheres of economy and party politics, it suffices to read or listen to the speeches made by the politicians, whatever their allegiances, to realize that their rhetoric is crammed with terms borrowed from the military vocabulary. In the age of semiotics, there are certain kinds of analysis which one is reluctant to undertake, because they would undermine some reassuring prejudices.

V

CENSURED WAR AND JUSTIFIED WAR

In what manner has war been judged? There is an apparent consensus that it has always been deplored as a scourge of human societies or as a moral evil. After all, it would not be difficult to find poems and long fragments in prose, going as far back as the ancient times, that praise the advantages and the benefits of peace. Here is a quotation from Ronsard's well-known 'exhortation': 'Peace fertilized the arid fields,/Peace under the yoke made the bulls bellow, /Peace inside the glens made the flocks jump'.[1]

Nonetheless, people have worshipped war as much, often for noble reasons, such as love of the homeland or the liberation of nations. In his book on censured war, Alain came to attribute this perpetual revival of war to the human passions which never reach a compromise.[2] This rather psychological explanation needs to be rounded off by the findings of modern biologists, that lay stress on human aggressiveness, a normal instinct necessary for the conservation of the group and the species, and which in particular circumstances may change into marked aggression. It should not be forgotten that war is a manifestation of violence and that human societies are founded on violence.[3] As long as human societies exist, the risk of the explosion of violence will persist. Violence may assume different forms, as the blood law, for instance, which is still the regulatory principle in certain communities, the vendetta, the revolt or the revolution, and the war. History shows that people have been able to preserve certain things by destroying others. Had everything been peacefully accumulated from the beginnings, mankind would have drowned in the clutter.

A coherent and congruent judgment of warfare bears on two kinds of war: the war of conquest and the war of independence. In this way, civil wars are left out, while only those conflicts that set cities, empires or nations one against the other are considered. A nation may try to subject one or several nations to its will, as a hegemony, or through colonization, occupation or annexation for various reasons, which may be economic, religious or purely political. On the other hand, a subjected nation may try to recover its independence in order to master its destiny alone. If that is the case, we need first to reject as unfounded some current and thoughtless opinions.

One of them claims that the very presence of armed forces is cause for war, and as a consequence, in order to make peace prevail, it is necessary to start demolishing such criminal institutions as military head-quarters. Guerrilla warfare may alone serve as a refutation of this opinion, because generally speaking, it is started by civilians and irregulars who take up arms and wage war to press on their political will of independence. When people want to wage war, they set up an army even there where there was none before. Another ungrounded opinion is that warfare is inherent in certain power structures but not in others. In reality, the democracies have always waged wars as have the monocracies, whether they have been monarchies, despotisms or dictatorships. Moreover, there is no specifically democratic way of waging war. Quite the opposite: war is not linked to any particular régime or power structure, but is part and parcel of politics as such. It is an expression of policy when the latter encounters resistance on its way. The third refutable opinion is the illusion of the 'irenocrats', as Alain used to call them, that is to say, those pacifists who believe that war may be avoided by trying to find a legal solution to the conflict. Is it necessary to remark with Jean-Jacques Rousseau that 'war is born out of peace, or at least, out of the precautions which people have taken in order to secure a lasting peace'?[4] Law can but acknowledge the legality of a state of fact that is the result of multiple wars. On the other hand, some people may regard the situation as unjust, and in consequence, would want to correct it, even at the cost of another war. The mistake is to think that law is essentially 'irenical'. Actually, it may be 'belligerent', too, in the same way as religion, the arts or the economy. In the case of conflict, law is generally used as a pretext of it.

By and large, such opinions have a common source: a faulty idea of peace, morally generous, without question, but practically inoperative. As a matter of fact, peace is held to be a state, a condition, in itself, independent of war and politics, as if it could be established regardless of the social conditions extant at the time. It is regarded as a kind of heavenly gift which could be bestowed on us simply because we desire it so much. Yet, war and peace have to be thought of together, because each in part is the work of politics. In other words, the illusion lies in the belief that only war is related to politics and that peace is a non-political state. In real life, there are the same governments that wage war and make peace. Hence peace does not in the least mean the abolition or the exclusion of the enemy, but rather it demands the recognition of the enemy. Said differently, peace is concluded with the enemy whom one fought during the war.

After all, with whom is peace to be made, if not with the enemy? There is no reason to conclude it with one's friend, because by definition, friendship is a state of peace. Thus peace is as political a matter as warfare is, because each in part presupposes the notion of enemy. On the other hand, it would be as mistaken to envisage peace as an absence of conflict. The difference between war and peace rests in the fact that in the case of peace, one does not seek to solve the eventual conflict(s) by resorting to armed violence. Because it is a consequence of politics and is dependent on the balance of power prevalent at the time, peace too may happen to be unjust. In any case, it is not the good in itself, in an eschatological sense, but the result of negotiations, recorded in a peace treaty. Only that kind of thinking that ignores the weight of the political action may desire peace in general or in the absolute sense, outside any peace treaty.

By holding onto an angelical notion of peace, so to speak, one succeeds in justifying war ideologically. Indeed, at all times, those who have undertaken such an enterprise would put forward several arguments in favour of warfare. Nevertheless, they would legitimize only that particular war which they themselves would undertake, and in rest, would remain content to condemn warfare both morally and literally as a calamity, unlike the idyllic hope of peace. What is new since the emergence of ideological thinking is the justification of war as such.

Thus Joseph de Maistre considered war 'divine in itself, because it is a law of the world'.[5] His contemporary, Juan Donoso Cortés saw in it a human fact, necessary eternal...a divine action.[6] As already seen, Proudhon found in warfare 'a manifestation of justice', because for him it was not a bestial action, but one of humanity.[7] Ruskin, on his part, saw in warfare a necessary form of education,[8] while Dostoevki held it to be a source of refreshment, of renewal of mankind.[9] More recently, René Quinton stressed the beauty and virility of warfare,[10] while Oswald Spengler interpreted it as the creator of all things great.[11] Ernest Jünger, in his turn, saw in warfare the way to a full and total existence.[12] Other writers, who are considered more moderate, however, could not help finding certain positive things in warfare. Kant has already been quoted. Hegel, on the other hand, found warfare indispensable for the moral development of mankind,[13] and so did Tocqueville who admitted that war always lifts the minds and the hearts of the people.[14] Indeed, all these opinions are apologies, that is to say, personal defences of warfare that had but an indirect impact on the course of events. In other words, these individual opinions are of more interest to the history of ideas than to the history of collective movements that took to violence and warfare with no hesitation, in order to secure the victory of their ideologies.

The justifications of which I would like to speak in particular have had an impact on social communities, primarily in virtue of their political and legal nature, without however ignoring their references to morality and religion. This kind of justification found its first pregnant formulation in the debates about just and unjust wars. By and large, these debates do not condemn war as such, but only some of its aspects. The debates actually started in the Middle Ages, among theologians and jurists, at a time when despite its evangelical principles, the Church found itself confronted by the persistence of wars, some of which being waged under its sponsorship. A lot has been written on the subject, beginning with the consilia evangelica, which would codify the feudal knight's rights and duties, and going on to the more modern works of the like of Francisco de Vittoria, Grotius and Vattel. Although this is not the place to review the theories of the just war and examine them critically, a point in their evolution is worth stressing, though, and which was first made evident by Carl Schmitt, namely the transition from the idea of the just war in virtue of the just cause of war,[15] to the just war carried on against the right enemy.[16]

Both these kinds of theory accept the idea of warfare, yet they introduce a distinction on the basis of the legitimacy of some of them, and of the illegitimacy of others.

In fact, our age is paradoxically characterized by a system of war justifications that lies behind an apparent pacifist will. The latter plays on two planes: one, that of the just cause, and the other, of the right enemy, without caring in the least about the subsequent confusion that occurs both theoretically and practically. Actually, if one takes either of these theses to their logical conclusion,

they lead to the same outcome. Oldendorp, one of the six-
teenth-century Lutheran jurists who upheld the just cause
theory, used to say that a just war was ultimately no war,
but the work of justice, whereas the unjust war was no war
either, but a rebellion against the just order.[17] Thus verbal
dialectic finally does away with the act of war. A modern
jurist, who is a supporter of the right enemy theory, would
reach a similar conclusion. In his eyes, war becomes 'an international crime' to the extent that all opposition to a
belligerent power is no longer war but police action, juridically founded and proper. Thus we find ourselves at the core
of the question of justifications which discredit present-
day political analyses: they no longer acknowledge the war
phenomenon sociologically, but transform warfare into a
punishment inflicted upon the enemy in the name of an allegedly moralizing justice.

We are far from the limitations to which warfare was sub-
mitted during the age of State wars which acquiesced in the
fact that either belligerent were just enemies: bellum
utrimque justum. The mutual acquiescence in the righteousness
of the cause of each led to what Proudhon came to call 'war
in form'.[18] In other words, the refusal to discriminate between a just and an unjust enemy, because both belligerents
fight for a cause that is defensible from the point of view
of law and morality, has so far been the condition of the hu-
manization and limitation of warfare. It has made both combat and its effects more moderate, and induced respect for
treaties on an international level. On the other hand, those
theories that try to draw a distinction between just and unjust wars help to intensify war to such a degree that renders it ever more frightening and implacable, because they
consistently discredit one of the adversaries either reli-
giously, morally or juridically. The discrimination between
enemies has led to the representation of war as criminal. At
the limit, there would be two kinds of war, one just and the
other unjust, two wholly different phenomena, that juridically
cannot be subsumed to the same concept of warfare.[19] The result is that by rendering war criminal, peace is rendered
criminal, too, because the mutual recognition of the enemies,
without which no peace treaty can be concluded, is no longer
possible. Such morally generous ideas as those grounded on
human rights may have nefarrious, even catastrophic effects

on politics, which whether one likes it or not, is pervaded
by power relationships that in their turn nullify the original generosity.

Let us take an example of justification of warfare: the
revolutionary ideology. At the beginning, the revolution
assumed a noble cause as its objective, namely, the liberation of the people from under a despotic yoke, or more
generally, the universal emancipation of mankind under the
auspices of class struggle. As soon as one examines the concrete evolution of historical facts, one discovers that revolution has become the modern means of justifying warfare.
As a matter of fact, given the widespread dissemination of
the revolutionary ideology in intellectual and other circles,
it has become important to one of the two camps in conflict
that it should pass for revolutionary, because by one and the
same blow its cause becomes just and sacred, whatever the
means it uses and regardless of the foreseeable consequences,
such as the replacement of the old regime by another, more
dictatorial and tyrannical. The list is long, of those rev-
olutions that brought to power implacable regimes, and so far
there are no exceptions. Nonetheless, all these wars have
enjoyed the support and the favours extended by the intel-
lectuals, whether they have taken place in Russia, Cuba,
Vietnam, Cambodia, or elsewhere. That has been so, because
everywhere they claim to be revolutionary wars. In politics,
one needs to think as Machiavelli, in order to understand the
Machiavellism which exploits the ideological generosity, that
is revolutionary in our times, for ends that have nothing
generous about them. It is by adopting this Machiavellian
point of view, which historically was a first step in the
direction of positive political thinking, that one is able to
grasp the fact that revolution has become a way to justify
warfare at present. By its very nature, revolution is a
violent, war-like action, the objective of which is not peace,
as far as peace rests in the recognition of the enemy, because it promotes the physical extermination not only of the
enemy, but also of the mere oppositionist. Thus, among all
the justifications of war that reject the distinction in order to be able more completely to make a criminal out of the
enemy, it is the most radical, because it denies to the enemy
his very existence. Pushed to that extreme, it become in effect a negation of politics as an activity that organizes

the cohabitation of people with different, and at times
divergent, interests and ideas.

It is with the enemy that one must make peace, because
after all, one wages war against him. As a result, the enemy
is a central concept of both states, that of war, as well as
that of peace. The millstone of the various brands of pacifism is the ignorance of this fundamental fact of reality.
Peace is not absolute, something in itself, independent of
social and historical circumstances. One may draw the necessary conclusions, one of which, at least, seems capital. It
is not possible to work out a peace doctrine in the absence
of a theory of war, as Proudhon himself would have said.
Hence, peace as the cradle of justice and happiness, in the
absence of all conflict, should not be opposed to war considered the cradle of all iniquities and misfortunes. It was
Dostoevski who wrote that the cause of war was bourgeois
peace.[20] Why is the state of peace abandoned in order to enter
a state of war, unless one thinks the peace unjust? In fact,
the stakes are political in either state. Both are situations
that depend upon a political will. The kind of peace that
exists in each period finds itself correlated with the
kind of war that is waged. There is no unique peace model,
which is to say that war may generate oppositions among
doctrines that all proclaim themselves pacifist, or at least
desirous of peace under certain conditions. It is easy to
imagine the existence of different kinds of peace as one does
in the case of war: peace through fear or deterrence, the
hegemonical peace of an imperialist or a federalist character, the ballanced peace attained through the respect of
power relations and of international rules, and so on. That
is also to say that peace too may be grounded in violence.
There are peaceful states as hard to tolerate as warfare.
The social questions cannot be solved in a Manichean manner.

NOTES

INTRODUCTION

1.   See 'L'État de Guerre' (Fragments) in THE POLITICAL WRITINGS OF JEAN-JACQUES ROUSSEAU, vol.I, New York, 1971 c 1915, p. 300. The original title of the Fragments had been 'Que l'état de guerre naît de l'état social'(The State of War is Generated by the Social Conditions), but eventually Rousseau cancelled it himself.

2.   Proudhon, Pierre Joseph: PHÉNOMÉNOLOGIE DE LA GUERRE, Book I, Ch. 2: 'La guerre est un fait divin', Paris, 1927 c1861, pp.31-32.

3.   JEREMIAH 8:10-11.

SOME ESSENTIAL REMARKS

1.   Cicero, Marcus Tullius (106-43 BC), Roman lawyer and politician, orator and thinker. See his PHILIPPIC VIII i.4, in CICERO: PHILIPPICS, Cambridge MA, 1969 c1919, pp.366-367.

2.   See LA GUERRE ET LA PAIX, vol. VI of OEUVRES COMPLETS DE P.-J. PROUDHON, Paris, 1927, pp.63-64.

3.   Schmitt, Carl: THE CONCEPT OF THE POLITICAL, Chicago, 1995, pp.28-29.

4.   Rousseau, op. cit., pp. 300-301.

5.   Clausewitz, Carl von: ON WAR, Princeton, 1976, p. 87.

6.   Clausewitz, op. cit., p. 227.

7.   Fénelon, François de Salignac de la Mothe- (1651-1715), French ecclesiastic and writer, was a vehement critic of Louis XIV's war policies, and an advocate of a quietist doctrine that was condemned by the Roman Catholic Church. He incurred the king's displeasure and had to retire to his diocese at Cambrai, after a formal submission to the Church.

8.   Kant, Emmanuel (1724-1804), German philosopher. See his CRITIQUE OF JUDGMENT, Part I: 'Critique of Aesthetic Judgment,' Indianapolis, 1987, p. 122. As it will be shown later on, Dostoevski shared his opinion on the nefarious effects of bourgeois peace.

9.   See Stegemann, Hermann: DER KRIEG, SEIN WESEN UND SEINE WAND-
     LUNG, vol. I, Stuttgart, 1939, p. 6.

10. See Kant, Emmanuel: CRITIQUE OF JUDGMENT. Part II, Indiana-
     polis, 1987, pp. 320-321. The Puhar translation, referred to
     here, rendered the notion as 'unintentional human endeavour'.

THE MODERN NOTION OF WAR

1.   The original French title of Baron Antoine de Jomini's book is
     PRÉCIS DE L'ART DE LA GUERRE (1836).

2.   See Preface ot MY REVERIES UPON THE ART OF WAR by Marshal
     Maurice de Saxe, in ROOTS OF STRATEGY, ed. by T.R. Phillips,
     Harrisburg, 1985 c1940, p. 189.

3.   Clausewitz, op. cit., pp. 66 and 71. The reference is to the
     preface written by Clausewitz's widow, who describes his efforts
     as having been aimed at a scientific understanding of the
     phenomenon of war, as well as to Clausewitz's own unfinished
     note of 1830, in which he writes about the difficulties of
     working out a scientific theory of the art of war.

4.   Bouthoul, Gaston (1896-1980), French social scientist, was
     founder of the Institute of Polemology in Paris and author of
     several works on various aspects of warfare, among which a hefty
     treatise on the sociology of war.

5.   The Iconoclasts were a religious sect that objected to the
     worship of images (icons), invoking among other things the pro-
     hibition in the Decalogue (Ex. 20:4), and idolatry as a poten-
     tial. Their influence peaked in the first quarter of the eighth
     century, when the use of icons was officially prohibited in the
     Byzantine Empire. The cult was restored half a century later
     by the seventh ecumenical council at Nicaea. A second iconoclas-
     tic period followed in the first half of the ninth century,
     which ended after the death of Emperor Theophilus (842 AD), when
     his widow restored icon worship for good.

6.   Clausewitz, op. cit., pp.101-102.

7.   Originally published as DAS VOLK IM WAFFEN, it was translated
     into English and published in London, fourteen years later, in
     1887. Its author (1843-1916) was a career German officer who
     took part in the Franco-Prussian war, and later on reorganized
     the Turkish armed forces on a modern basis. Von der Goltz died
     of cholera in the Middle East during WWI. Ludendorff, Erich
     (1865-1937), German general, chief of staff of the German army,
     had a decisive role in the way Germany waged the 1914-1918 war.
     Subsequently, he tried to draw some strategical lessons from
     that experience, and consequently was regarded as the theoreti-
     cian of modern total war, and in particular of WWII.

8.   Weber, Max (1864-1920), German jurist, economist and sociolo-
     gist; see his ECONOMY AND SOCIETY, New York, 1968, pp.24-26 and
     941-958.

9.   Pareto, Vilfredo (1848-1923), Italian civil engineer, econo-
     mist and sociologist, one of the classics of modern social
     sciences; see his MIND AND SOCIETY: A TREATISE ON GENERAL
     SOCIOLOGY, vol.I, section 60, New York, 1935, pp.86-87.

10. LETTRE OUVERTE AUX PACIFISTES, Paris, 1972, p. 25.

11. See the article 'Une armée de la paix reste une armée' in the
     review GUERRES ET PAIX, No. 4, Paris, 1967.

12. Hans Delbrück writes about strategies of attrition and of an-
     nihilation, respectively. See his HISTORY OF THE ART OF WAR
     WITHIN THE FRAMEWORK OF POLITICAL HISTORY, Vol. IV, Westport
     Conn., 1985, pp. 108-109 and 439-444.

13. See Grousset, René: THE EMPIRE OF THE STEPPES, New Brunswick
     NJ, 1970.

14. This is a very approximate translation of the French phrase
     'lime sourde'. See Caillois, Roger: BELLONE OU LA PENTE DE LA
     GUERRE, Brussels, 1963, p.9.

15. Caillois, op. cit., p. 26.

16. Caillois, op. cit., pp. 35-56 and 237-244.

THE CONVENTIONAL ASPECTS OF WAR

1.   Lipsus, Justus (1547-1606) humanist and peripathetic scholar,
     born in Brabant, taught at various universities in Northern
     Europe and authored numerous works on a wide range of subject-
     matters, including politics, history, moral philosophy, criti-
     cism and archeology, enjoying much popularity in his time. King
     Philip II of Spain granted him the title of royal historiogra-
     pher, despite the fact that he changed his religious orienta-
     tion thrice during his life-time.

2.   See Machiavelli, Niccolo: THE ART OF WAR, Indianapolis, 1965,
     p. 4. Machiavelli (1469-1527) Tuscan humanist, historian,
     civil servant and politician, is best known for his treatise on
     practical politics, THE PRINCE (1513).

3.   Here Machiavelli follows closely Xenophon, the Greek general
     and ancient historian who in his CYROPAEDIA I.ii.9-10, regards
     hunting as the best training for war.

4.   Caillois, op. cit., p. 60.

5.   Caillois, op. cit., pp.59-61.

6.   Bodin, Jean (1529-1596), French jurist and economist, author

of a treatise on governance RES PUBLICA (The Commonwealth) published in 1578. In it he laid down the principles of a monarchy
working hand in hand with a representative body. Thus he lent a
basis to Henry IV's policy of appeasement and tolerance.

7.   Loisel, Antoine (1536-1617), French jurist and royal advocate,
     prolific author on such issues as tolerance,royal authority and
     sovereignty, and of a collection of rules, sentences and common
     sayings pertaining to the French common or customary law, enti-
     tled INSTITUTES COUTUMIÈRES, first published as an annexe to
     Cocquille's posthumous publication on the institutes of French
     law in 1608. Coquille, Guy (1523-1603), French jurist, also
     wrote a Dialogue upon France's misfortunes (1590), on the havoc
     caused by the wars of religion. Loyseau, Charles (1566-1627),
     advocate of the Paris Parliament, used his knowledge of Roman
     law to resolve difficult problems raised by the French customary
     law and wrote treatises on social ranks, public office, rent,
     mortgage and rural justice. Hobbes, Thomas (1588-1679), English
     political thinker, author of THE LEVIATHAN and DE CIVE.

8.   Richelieu, Armand Jean du Plessis, cardinal de (1585-1642),
     French statesman, defender of French absolute monarchy, which
     he actively promoted both in his foreign policy and in the
     administrative reforms which he undertook as the chief of the
     King's Council. See also Thuau, Etienne: RAISON D'ÉTAT ET PEN-
     SÉE POLITIQUES À L'ÉPOQUE DE RICHELIEU, Paris, 1966, pp. 9-
     12, 166-178 and 351-358.

9.   See Bodin, Jean: SIX BOOKS OF THE COMMONWEALTH, Book I,ch. 10,
     Oxford, 1955, pp. 27-30.

10. Ibid., pp. 44-45.

11. 'L'État c'est Moi!' The phrase is apocryphal, but it has been
     perpetuated in the way myths do, to express a state of mind
     that was prevalent both at the royal court and in the ranks of
     the administrative apparatus at the time.

12. Vauban, Sébastien Le Prestre, marquess of (1633-1707), French
     career officer and military writer, also known for various
     large-scale public works, reached the highest rank in the French
     army, that of marshal, only to fall foul of the royal authority
     with the publication of his draft of a financial reform of the
     realm, aware as he had become of the iniquity by which taxes
     were exacted from the people.

13. To these one may add the trench.

14. Lilburne, John (1614?-1657), an English commissioned officer
     at the outbreak of the Civil War, left the army in 1645 to be-
     come a political agitator and vocal critic of government under
     its various forms. Associated with the Levellers, he was among

the 1647 petitioners to the House of Commons as the supreme
authority of England, demanding the abolition of the House of
Lords and other constitutional and legal changes effective
immediately. On the other hand, 'the diggers'was the name given
by the authorities to a small party of men who began cultivat-
ing common waste land in Surrey, claiming that it was an un-
deniable equity that common people should cultivate and dwell
upon the commons, without paying any rent. One of their leaders
was Gerrard Winstanley whose period of fame lasted between
1648 and 1652, owing to the tracts, pamphlets and memorials
which he published on behalf and in defence of the Diggers.
Through them he disseminated communistic ideas and attacked the
official Christian beliefs and the ecclesiastical government,
thus revealing himself, in the process, a universalist.

15. Quoted by Johannes Ullrich in his LA GUERRE À TRAVERS LES
    ÂGES, Paris, 1942, pp. 183-184.

16. Groot, Hugo de, better known as Grotius (1583-1645), Dutch
    jurist, upholder of the theory of free seas, escaped from pri-
    son and took refuge in France during the religious conflicts
    in the Netherlands, where by his work DE JURE BELLI AC PACIS,
    he made his contribution to the foundation of modern interna-
    tional law.

17. Pufendorf, Samuel (1632-1694), German historian and jurist,
    a disciple of Grotius, had to seek refuge in Sweden against the
    defenders of tradition whom he had challenged by advocating
    freedom of conscience for everybody and a religion free of
    scholasticism. In his magnum opus, DE JURE NATURAE ET GENTIUM
    (1672), he supported natural law at the expense of the fragmen-
    tary and chaotic character of the law prevalent in the polit-
    ical entities of the Holy Empire, and generally known as the
    Germanic law.

18. Burlamaqui, Jean-Jacques (1694-1746), Geneva-born law profes-
    sor and jurist; his often reprinted PRINCIPLES OF POLITICAL LAW
    had been preceded by his PRINCIPLES OF NATURAL LAW (1747). His
    merit lies in the fact that he condensed and systematized the
    works of his predecessors in the field.

19. Vattel, Emmerich de (1714-1767), Swiss-born German political
    thinker and court councillor at Dresden. He is best known for
    his magnum opus DROIT DES GENS OU PRINCIPES DE LA LOI NATURELLE
    APPLIQUÉS À LA CONDUITE ET AUX AFFAIRES DES NATIONS ET DES
    SOUVERAINS (1758). There, the concepts of nation and of indi-
    vidual rights, as well as the relation between nation and
    religion are given priority over those of sovereign monarchy
    and the Catholic church. His ideas contributed to the ideologi-
    cal groundwork of the American and the French Revolutions, as
    well as of the modern total wars.

20. Vattel, Emmerich de: CIVIL LAW, Vol. II, Book III, 3:25, Washington DC, 1916, p. 21.

21. See Note to the article 'Critique', supplement of 1771 to Voltaire's DICTIONNAIRE PHILOSOPHIQUE, Paris, 1967, p. 502.

22. See Avant-Propos of 1746 and Avant-Propos of 1775 to OEUVRES HISTORIQUES DE FRÉDERIC II, ROI DE PRUSSE, Berlin, 1846, pp. vi-ix, xvi, xx and xxiii, respectively.

23. See Koselleck, Reinhart: CRITIQUE AND CRISIS, Cambridge Mass., 1988, pp. 98-123.

24. Louvois, François-Michel Le Tellier, Marquess of (1641-1691), minister of Louis XIV, followed his father as State Secretary for War in 1666, in which capacity he showed an unusual organizational talent. Moreover, he was a founder of colleges for artillery and military engineers, as well as of military colleges for nobles in border towns; introduced military uniforms, distinguishing the soldiers by regiments, and established service in the army as the main criterion for promotion within the ranks, at the expense of birth.

25. Folard, Jean-Charles de (1669-1752), a career officer, was also the first modern author of a book on guerrilla warfare, which unfortunately was never printed. Published in 1721, a time of peace, his NOUVELLES DÉCOUVERTES SUR LA GUERRE unfolds against the background provided by a modern translation of Polybus' HISTORY in six volumes brought out in Paris between 1717 and 1730.

26. There were indeed exceptions, too, particularly during the Seven Years' War (1756-1763).(Author's note)

27. Marivaudage is that kind of conversation that uses pretentious and contrived language resembling that of the plays written by the French playwright Pierre Carlet de Chamblain de Marivaux (1688-1763). See also Fisch, Jörg: KRIEG UND FRIEDEN IM FRIEDENSVERTRAG, Stuttgart, 1979, pp. 281-285 and 536-537.

28. That idea originated with Frederick II of Prussia, but Gribeauval, Jean-Baptiste Vaquette de (1715-1789), French-born career officer, military engineer and artillery expert, expanded and institutionalized it. The concept consisted in the reorganization and deployment of the artillery in conjunction with the the other branches of the armed forces. To that end, as general inspector of the artillery, Gribeauval took a series of steps to improve the design of and standardize all artillery pieces, as well as to secure the corresponding training of artillerymen in specially organized schools.

29. See Buchheit, Gert: VERNICHTUNGS ODER ERMATTUNGSSTRATEGIE? Berlin, 1942, p. 59.

30. Guibert, Hippolyte, count of (1743-1790), son of a French gen-
    eral, was made to experience the battle-field at 13; however,
    his attention focussed on military matters consistently only
    after his appointment as member and reporter on the administra-
    tive board of the Department of War in 1787. His ESSAI GÉNÉRAL
    DE TACTIQUE was first printed in London, in 1772, probably to
    avoid scandal and embarassment.

31. Printed in pamphlet form and distributed under the name of l'
    abbé Raynal, as a letter of 10th December, 1789, addressed to
    the National Assembly. Guibert's major works, but not the let-
    ter, have been edited by General Ménard and published as ÉCRITS
    MILITAIRES: 1772-1790, Paris,1977.

32. Unidentified. No copy of the letter was available at the
    time when the present translation was edited.

33. Custine, Adam Philippe, count of (1740-1793), French general,
    who had taken part in the American War of Independence, was ap-
    pointed Commander of the Army of the North, only to be beheaded
    soon after for not holding some of its territory. Dumouriez,
    Charles François du Périer (1739-1823), French general and
    foreign secretary in 1792, was discharged from his command by
    the Convention, but managed to join the opposition abroad
    and so escaped Custine's fate.

34. Professor Freund's definition of ideology is the following:
    'a totality of more or less coherent ideas, grounded in an emo-
    tional adhesion and capable of rallying its upholders to col-
    lective action'. See also p. 7 above.

35. See OEUVRES DE SAINT JUST, Paris, 1946, p. 145. The quotation
    is from the speech on the reorganization of the army made
    before the Convention on 12th February, 1793.

36. Ibid., p. 275.

37. Houchard, Jean Nicholas (1740-1793), French general of humble
    origin, joined the army at 15. A Lt-Colonel and a Knight of
    St. Louis at the time of the Revolution, he embraced the cause
    of the latter enthusiastically, and eventually was promoted to
    the rank of Lt-General, scored an outstanding victory at Hond-
    schoote on 9th September, 1793, by which he forced the British
    to lift the siege of Dunkirk and give up all plans to invade
    France by the Alliance. Not content with that result, the
    Committee of Public Safety arrested him and sent him before
    the Revolutionary Tribunal for not having destroyed the entire
    British army. Less than three months after his victory at the
    front, Houchard was sentenced to death and executed.

38. Quoted from Chateaubriand's MÉMOIRES D'OUTRE-TOMBE, Book XX,
    ch.10, by Caillois, op cit., p. 117.

39. See Clausewitz, op. cit., pp. 591-593.

40. Jomini, Henri de (1779-1869) had been a Swiss career officer
     before becoming chief of staff to Ney, the French Marshal.
     He was created French baron after the conclusion of the peace
     at Tilsit in 1807. Later on, vexed by the treatment he was
     receiving at the hands of another of Napoleon's marshals,
     Jomini joined the Russian army in 1813, attaining the rank of
     general.

41. The speech was delivered before the National Convention on 4th
     of February, 1794. See TEXTES CHOISIS DE ROBESPIERRE, Vol.III,
     Paris, 1974, p. 18.

42. Danton, Georges Jacques (1759-1794), Parisian advocate of peas-
     ant stock, founder of the Cordeliers' Club alongside Marat and
     Desmoulins, became minister of justice of the new republic. One
     of the original members of the Committee of Public Safety, Dan-
     ton became president of the Jacobin club after the downfall of
     the Girondists. His attempts to attenuate the ruthlessness of
     the Revolutionary Tribunal, a founder of which he had been, end-
     ed into his own death sentence on charges of conspiracy to over-
     throw the government during the reign of Terror. Hébert, Jacques
     René (1755-1794), former footman and Jacobin, became editor of
     the paper LE PÈRE DUCHESNE, a member of the revolutionary
     council and of the commission of inquiry set up to investigate
     Marie-Antoinette. He introduced the trumped-up charge of incest
     with her son against her, was instrumental into converting the
     Cathedral of Notre-Dame in Paris into a Temple of Reason, but
     eventually managed to displease Robespierre who had him sent to
     the guillotine. Babeuf, François (1760-1797) was in turn sent
     to the guillotine after it had been found out that he had taken
     part in a plot to overthrow the Directorate and replace it with
     an extreme democratic and communistic system of government.

43. See Letter No.143 of London, 20th July, 1870, in KARL MARX AND
     FREDERICK ENGELS: SELECTED CORRESPONDENCE, 1846-1895, New York,
     1942, p. 292.

44. See Letter No. 145 written by Engels to Marx from Manchester,
     on 15th August, 1870, ibid., p. 296.

45. Liebknecht, Wilhelm (1826-1900), German politician and founder
     of the Social-Democratic Party of that country in 1869.

46. Originally published in French as PAIX ET GUERRE ENTRE LES NA-
     TIONS, Paris, 1968, and PENSER LA GUERRE, Paris, 1976, respec-
     tively. The full titles of the English translations are: PEACE
     AND WAR: A THEORY OF INTERNATIONAL RELATIONS, New York, 1973,
     and CLAUSEWITZ, PHILOSOPHER OF WAR, London, 1983. Likewise, see
     Arnold, Theodor: DER REVOLUTIONÄRE KRIEG, Pfaffenhofen am
     Ilm, 1961, pp. 224-226.

47. See note 7, p. 69.

48. Clausewitz, op. cit., p. 582.

49. Foch, Ferdinand (1851-1929), French officer, instructor at the
     War College and founder of the French Centre of High Military
     Studies, was appointed Supreme Commander of the Allied Forces
     in March 1918. Joffre, Joseph (1852-1931), French officer,
     joined the French Corps of Engineers during the Franco-Prussian
     War, was promoted to Chief of the French General Headquarters
     in 1911 and made Generalissimo in 1914. Unable to break the
     German frontline, he was removed from his commanding post two
     years later, given the title of Marshal of France and sent on
     assignment to the United States. For a different view of the
     conflict between Foch and Joffre see Carrias, Eugène: LA PENSÉE
     MILITAIRE FRANCAISE, Paris, 1960, pp. 285-286, 296-298 and 305-
     307. According to Carrias, Foch and Joffre were not replicating
     the doctrinal conflict between Moltke and Schlieffen; rather
     their differences were focussed upon the necessity of military
     intelligence, discipline and initiative along the channel of
     command.

50. Moltke, Helmuth von (1800-1891), a lieutenant in the Danish ar-
     my, became staff officer at the Prussian General Headquarters,
     and revealed himself a gifted strategist in the wars against
     Austria and France, respectively. Moltke was created count and
     promoted to the rank of field-marshal at the end of the Franco-
     Prussian War. A Conservative member of the Reichstag from
     1867 until his death. Schlieffen, Alfred von (1833-1913), Ger-
     man staff officer during the Franco-Prussian War, Chief of the
     General Staff after 1891, and field-marshal in 1911, outlined
     the new strategy that was put into practice by Germany at the
     beginning of WWI. See Aron, Raymond: CLAUSEWITZ, PHILOSOPHER OF
     WAR, Englewood Cliffs, 1985, pp. 252-253 and 256-257, and
     Ritter, Gerhard: THE SWORD AND THE SCEPTER, vol. II, Coral
     Gables, 1970, pp. 196-206. See also Carrias, Eugène: LA PENSÉE
     MILITAIRE ALLEMANDE, Paris, 1948, pp. 306-321.

51. Carrias, ibid., pp. 238-252, 291-295.

52. The former has never been translated into English. Its title
     may be rendered as 'War Leadership and Politics'. The latter,
     though, was translated and published in English in London in
     1936, under the title THE NATION AT WAR.

53. During the latter half of the second century B.C..

54. Quoted from Schmitt, Carl: THEORIE DES PARTISANEN, Berlin, 1975,
     p. 20.

55. See, for instance, the chapter entitled 'People's War' in the
     treatise ON WAR.

56. See Lenin, V.I.: WHAT IS TO BE DONE?, London, 1988, pp. 229ff.

57. See the anthology compiled by Mauro Armiño: LA LUCHA DE GUER-
RILLAS, SEGUN LOS CLASICOS DEL MARXISMO-LENINISMO,Madrid, 1980.

58. See, for instance, the discussion between Raymond Aron and
Carl Schmitt,partially reproduced in Aron's CLAUSEWITZ, PHILOS-
OPHER OF WAR, Englewood Cliffs, 1985, pp. 364-365.

59. Doly, Guy: STRATÉGIE FRANCE-ÉUROPE: SÉCURITÉ DE LA FRANCE ET
UNION EUROPÉENNE, Paris, 1977, pp. 77-78.

60. Quoted from Doly, op. cit., p.27.

61. See Armiño, op. cit., pp. 173-176 and 182-183.

62. See Schmitt, Carl: DER NOMOS DER ERDE IM VÖLKERRECHT DES JUS
PUBLICUM EUROPAEUM, Cologne, 1950, pp. 112-184.

63. So far no peace treaty has been concluded with Germany. What
was signed in Moscow, on the 12th September, 1990, was only a
treaty on the Final Measures regarding unification and the end-
ing of all remaining occupation rights of the WWII Allies
within the German boundaries drawn in 1945, after Germany's
capitulation. In other words, a legal formula was provided for
the termination of Allied military occupation of the territory
that was not annexed by any other country after the German
capitulation.

EVOLVING TECHNICAL ASPECTS OF WARFARE

1. See note 15, page 72 above.

2. For a different English translation of this quotation see
Maistre, Joseph de: ST PETERSBURG: DIALOGUES OR CONVERSATIONS
ON THE TEMPORAL GOVERNMENT OF PROVIDENCE, Seventh Dialogue,
Montreal, 1993, p. 215.

3. Caillois, op. cit., p. 116.

4. Here we leave aside the conditions of those city-states that
also happened to the naval powers. (Author's note)

5. Epaminondas (420 BC? - 362 BC), Theban general and politician,
came to the fore after the liberation of his polis from Spartan
occupation. Throughout the rest of his life, he did not spare
his talents to contain Sparta's expansionist tendencies, break
Athens' naval supremacy and make Thebe the most important land
power among the Greek city-states. His death in battle brought
to an abrupt end Thebe's political ambitions of greatness.

6. Philip II (383 BC - 336 BC), king of Macedonia, had been a
hostage of Thebe in Epaminondas' time, successfully embarked
upon the conquest of the Greek city-states, while reorganizing

his armed forces in the process, in keeping with the new conditions. Alexander (356 BC - 323 BC), king of Macedonia, son
of the former, pupil of Aristoteles, put in practice the expansionist intentions of his father, organized a Pan-Hellenic
expedition against the Persians that resulted in the occupation
of the entire Middle East up to the Hindus Valley and of Egypt.

7.   Diadochs or 'successors', Greek term referring to Alexander's
chief lieutenants who tried to partition his empire among themselves, after his death in 323 BC. After almost half a century
of constant war among the diadochs, the boundaries of the
various Hellenistic states were settled, thus putting an end
to the ambition of holding Alexander's empire together as one
political entity.

8.   Belisarius (500 AD? - 565 AD) and Narses (d. 574 AD).

9.   See Hirsch, Paul, ed.: WIDUKINDS SÄCHSISCHE GESCHICHTEN, New
York, 1965, c1931, pp. 49-54. There is no English translation
of the entire work.

10.   Widukind's explanation seems more pertinent by far, after all,
he had been a contemporary of the events, than Marx's famous
formula:'the handmill gives you society with the feudal lord;
the steam-mill, society with the industrial capitalist.' (Author's note.) See also Marx, Karl: THE POVERTY OF PHILOSOPHY,
New York, 1992, p. 81.

11.   See p. 28 above.

12.   Ullrich, op. cit., p. 116.

13.   The franc-tireur corps of WWI prefigured them. (Author's note)

14.   Gribeauval won the approval of the War Department and of the
Commission of Marshals in 1774 to equip the French army with a
variety of standardized cannons, in keeping with the nature of
anticipated operations and the terrain, and in the exclusive
care of specialized artillery officers. See also Carrias,
op. cit., Paris, 1960, pp. 176-177.

15.   In 480 BC, Leonidas, at the head of a contingent of the allied
Greek armies, had the task of holding the Pass of Thermopylae,
in Central Greece, against the invading Persians.

16.   See Xenophon, op. cit., I, vi.14-15.

17.   Athenian general and politician (450 BC? - 404 BC).

18.   Duke of Saxony and Germanic king (876? - 936) prepared the
social, political, economic and military conditions that rendered possible the formation of a Germanic empire under his
son, Otto the Great.

19.   See Machiavelli: THE PRINCE, ch. 13, Oxford, 1987, p. 47.

20. Unidentified.

21. Feuquière, Antoine de Pas, marquess of (1648-1711), French
     general, author of MÉMOIRES SUR LA GUERRE, printed posthumously
     at Amsterdam in 1731. For Folard, Jean Charles de (1669-1752),
     see note 25, p. 73 above. Lloyd, Henry (1720?-1783), Welsh-
     born military engineer and officer, author of A POLITICAL AND
     MILITARY RHAPSODY ON THE DEFENCE OF GREAT BRITAIN (1779), as
     well as of an unfinished history of the Seven-Year War,entitled
     HISTORY OF THE WAR BETWEEN THE KING OF PRUSSIA AND THE EMPRESS
     OF GERMANY AND HER ALLIES (1766-1782).

22. Chambray's PHILOSOPHIE DE LA GUERRE was published in 1827,
     yet he kept on writing about various aspects of warfare, after-
     wards. He had started his career as artillery sublieutenant
     in 1801. Taken prisoner by the Russians during Napoleon's Rus-
     sian campaign, he compiled the first draft of his important
     work, HISTOIRE DE L'ÉXPEDITION DE RUSSIE, while in captivity.
     For Jomini, see note 40, p. 75 above. He wrote extensively on
     historical and military matters, though his best-known single
     work is his PRÉCIS DE L'ART DE LA GUERRE, translated into sev-
     eral languages.

23. See Jomini, PRÉCIS DE L'ART DE LA GUERRE, Paris, 1977, p. 14.
     The available English translation could not be used here be-
     cause it renders obscure the point made by Professor Freund re-
     garding Jomini's premise.

24. See ed. cit., chs. I and II, and particularly pp. 19-24,49,63,
     70 and 77.

25. The original German text was first printed in 1937. There is
     no English translation of this text. Professor Freund refers
     to a French translation included in a selection of letters and
     shorter writings by Clausewitz, and published under the title
     DE LA REVOLUTION À LA RESTAURATION, Paris, 1976, p. 45. More
     recently, the original German text was reproduced as 'Strategie
     aus dem Jahre 1804 mit Zusätzen von 1808 und 1809' in Clause-
     witz's VERSTREUTE KLEINE SCHRIFTEN, Osnabrück, 1979. For the
     definition given by Clausewitz see p. 33 of this edition.

26. Liddell-Hart, Sir Basil (1895-1970), British military historian
     whose best-known work is STRATEGY: THE INDIRECT APPROACH,
     in six revised editions between 1923 and 1967.Cluseret, Gustave
     Paul (1823-1900), career officer, politician and businessman,
     joined Garibaldi during the struggle for independence, and then,
     the North in the American Civil War; there he reached the rank
     of general and was naturalized American. Resigned from the
     Northern Army in protest against General Milroy's treatment of
     civilians, founded the radical journal, THE NEW NATION,attached
     himself to the Fenian movement, took refuge back in France

where his attacks against Napoleon III's administration even
tually landed him in prison. There, he came into contact with
members of the International and joined their group. In order
to avoid another arrest, he invoked his American citizenship
and had to return to New York. Wrote articles on the reorganization of the French army, returned to France in September1870,
and took a stand against the French Government of National
Defence when denied a commanding post in the French Army.
Joined Bakunin, set up a short-lived revolutionary commune at
Marseille and eventually became a member of the Paris Commune.
Later, he was arrested and interned on suspicion of treason,
as a scapegoat for the Communards' failure to withstand the
counterattacks of the Versailles army, but managed to escape.

27. See in particular Doly, op. cit., pp.13-82.

28. Mackinder,Sir Halford (1861-1947), British geographer, explor-
er and politician, author of BRITAIN AND BRITISH SEAS (1902).
His theory of the heartland as a natural seat of power, which
he expounded in his article 'The Geographical Pivot of History'
(1904), eventually became better known to the students of the
Geopolitik in Germany than to those in his own country. Ratzel,
Friedrich (1844-1904), German geographer,a pioneer in the field
of geography as the study of the relationships of the human
being and its surroundings. His most important works were
POLITISCHE GEOGRAPHIE (1897) and DIE ERDE UND DAS LEBEN (1901-
1902). Vidal de la Blanche, Paul (1845-1918), French geographer
and author of PRINCIPES DE GÉOGRAPHIE HUMAINE, published post-
posthumously.

29. See Célérier, Pierre: GÉOPOLITIQUE ET GÉOSTRATÉGIE, Paris,
1955, pp. 5, 74-88.

30. See Bouthoul, Gaston: TRAITÉ DE POLÉMOLOGIE, Paris, 1970
pp.330-340.

31. The distinction between capitalist and socialist economies is
not as dated as some would like to believe in 1996, for instance, in the aftermath of the suppression of the terms 'the
cold war' from the parlance of international politics (end of
year 1989). Their doctrines are still not only in circulation,
but also, and sometimes furiously, put into practice, rallying
supporters in a variety of camps whether governmental or not.
Rathenau, Walter (1867-1922), German industrialist of Jewish
origin, was appointed head of the Office for Raw Materials during WWI, in which position he was able to develop and apply
his principles of redistribution, by setting priorities for the
exploitation of the country's resources in keeping with the war
interests.

32. See, for instance, Tavel, Charles H.: THE THIRD INDUSTRIAL AGE

- STRATEGY FOR BUSINESS SURVIVAL, Oxford, 1980.

33. Lenin, op. cit., p. 235n.

CENSURED WAR AND JUSTIFIED WAR

1.   'La paix fertilisa les campagnes steriles,/'La paix dessous le joug fist mugir les toreaux,/'La paix dedans les prez fist sauter les troupeaux,/...' from 'Exhortation pour la Paix' in OEUVRES COMPLÈTES, vol. II, Paris, 1950, p. 441.

2.   See Chartier, Émile (Alain): MARS OU LA GUERRE JUGÉE, Paris, 1969, c1936, especially pp. 81-98. This work has not been translated into English.

3.   See Maffesoli, Michel and Passin, Alain: LA VIOLENCE FONDA-TRICE, Paris, 1978, pp. 24-28, 31-40.

4.   See note 1, p. 68.

5.   See ST PETERSBURG DIALOGUES, loc. cit., pp. 218-219.

6.   Source not identified. Donoso-Cortès, Juan (1809-1853), Spanish politician and diplomat of Roman-Catholic orientation. As a practical politician, Donoso saw in war a means of establishing an international balance of power, since victory, as its objective, was prone to set up a hierarchy among the nations vying for power.

7.   Proudhon, op. cit., pp. 55-56.

8.   See Ruskin, John: THE CROWN OF WILD OLIVE, New York, 1910, p. 80.

9.   Dostoïevski: JOURNAL D'UN ÉCRIVAIN, Paris, 1972, pp. 509 and 511.

10. Quinton, René (1866-1925), French physiologist and artillery officer during WWI, authored a collection of aphorisms, MAXIMES SUR LA GUERRE (Paris, 1930), in which one comes across such sentences as 'war is the natural state of the males of the species' (p.18), 'war is a chapter of love' (p.22), or 'war is the noble mode of human activity' (p.58).

11. See DECLINE OF THE WEST, vol. II, New York, 1981, p. 363.

12. Particularly in his book DER KAMPF ALS INNERES ERLEBNISS (1922). See also Caillois, op. cit., pp. 179-184.

13. See his PHILOSOPHY OF RIGHT, Part 3, ch. 2, par. 324, Oxford, 1952, pp. 209-210, and his PHENOMENOLOGY OF SPIRIT, VI,A(b), par. 475, Oxford, 1977, pp.288-289.

14. 'I do not wish to speak ill of war; war almost always widens a nation's mental horizons and raises its heart', in DEMOCRACY IN

AMERICA, vol. II, New York, 1966, p. 624.

15. As translated from the Latin justa causa belli.

16. In Latin in the original text: justus hostis. It means the
     indisputable, legitimate enemy. In his book CARL SCHMITT:
     POLITICS AND THEORY (West Port, 1990), Paul Edward Gottfried,
     on the other hand, translates the same terms as 'appropriate
     enemy'. See Schmitt, Carl: DIE WENDUNG ZUM DISKRIMINIERDEN
     KRIEGSBEGRIFF (For a Conceptualization of War by Means of
     Discrimination), Munich, 1938.

17. Oldendorp, Johannes (1480?-1567),German jurist and law profes-
     sor, supporter of the spread of the Reformation in Northern
     Germany. His ideas on war are included in his annotations to the
     First Book of the Pandecta and in his Exposition in leges XII
     tabularum, particularly in the chapters De Bello Publico et
     Privato and Duella iusta, all in COLLECTED WORKS OF IOANNIS
     OLDENDORPII, Aarlen, 1966, pp. 14 and 43.

18. Proudhon entitled the third book of his work LA GUERRE ET LA
     PAIX, 'La guerre dans les formes' after Vattel.

19. See Schmitt, Carl, op. cit., Munich, 1938. (Author's note)

20. Dostoïevski, op. cit., Paris, 1972, p. 976.

INDEX